Contents

"Innovation is the ability to see change as
an opportunity - not a threat."

— Steve Jobs

1. Introduction to the Cosmic Role of Linux in Space

In the rapidly evolving landscape of technology and science, our journey into the final frontier is no longer just a dream but a tangible pursuit. As we set our sights on Mars, aiming to make it our second home, it becomes imperative to consider the technological backbone that will support this venture. One paramount component of this journey is the operating systems that will govern our machines, tools, and communications in such extreme environments.

Linux, known for its open-source nature and flexibility, emerges as a crucial player in this field. This book, 'Linux on Mars: Preparing OS Systems for Space Exploration', embarks on a detailed exploration of how this robust operating system is being fine-tuned and tailored to meet the unique challenges posed by interplanetary expeditions.

Readers will gain insights into the adaptations required for an OS to function efficiently on Mars, where environmental conditions are nothing like those on Earth. As we delve into technical intricacies and strategic planning, this book serves both as a guide and a motivator for tech enthusiasts, developers, and space explorers, presenting a roadmap of how Linux is poised to revolutionize our approach to space exploration. With a pragmatic and down-to-earth approach, this introductory chapter lays the foundation for the intricate journey that follows, ensuring that all readers, regardless of their technical background, grasp the profound intersection of technology and space travel.

2. The Importance of Operating Systems in Space Missions

2.1. Historical Context of Operating Systems in Space

The history of operating systems in space is a fascinating journey that mirrors the rapid advancements of technology and our unyielding quest to explore beyond our planet. In the early days of space exploration, the technological landscape was rudimentary, and the challenges of developing systems that could operate reliably in the harsh vacuum of space were immense. The prevailing operating systems during the first era of space missions were hardware-centric and typically developed in isolation, often tightly-bound to the specific platforms they were intended to control.

In the 1960s, space missions were governed by systems that could hardly be equated with the modern concept of an operating system. The Apollo Guidance Computer (AGC), famously used in NASA's Apollo missions, was revolutionary for its time. Developed by MIT Instrumentation Laboratory, the AGC operated on a simple executive system designed for real-time operations. The AGC's software utilized a very specific assembly language tailored for its exclusive hardware, exhibiting a tightly configured architecture that modern engineers would find restricting. Despite its limitations, the AGC was groundbreaking, demonstrating the potential for computers in space navigation and control.

As technology progressed, so too did the complexity of space missions. The 1970s and 1980s saw increased reliance on microprocessors and the nascent field of software engineering, giving rise to increasingly sophisticated embedded operating systems. The use of real-time operating systems (RTOS) became essential as missions like Skylab and the Space Shuttle required not only navigation and guidance but also data handling, scientific analysis, and even on-board diagnostics in the event of system failures. These RTOS systems were often custom-built for particular spacecraft and included multi-tasking capabilities, allowing various processes to occur simultaneously—an absolute necessity when managing multiple systems in the harsh environment of space.

The International Space Station (ISS), launched in the late 1990s, represented a paradigm shift in how operating systems were viewed in the context of space missions. Operating systems were no longer just simplistic responses to input; they had to manage complex interactions in a modular environment where various international partners collaborated. The need for standardization began to emerge as a critical focus. The ISS utilized a variety of systems for different applications, many of which were based on UNIX-like architectures due to their robustness, adaptability, and support for multi-user environments.

As we moved into the 21st century, the rise of open-source solutions began to reshape the operational dynamics of space systems. The ability to customize and share software within the aerospace community allowed for collaborative developments that enhanced reliability and diminished costs. The European Space Agency's use of the Linux operating system for several of its satellites is a notable instance of this trend. Linux's modular design, straightforward maintenance, and open-source nature make it ideal for the evolving technological landscape of space exploration.

Additionally, with a greater emphasis on in-situ resource utilization and advanced automation, as seen with missions like the Mars Rover, the software requirements became more complex. These systems demanded operating environments capable of significant adaptability, particularly since rovers operate independently for extended periods, requiring autonomy in navigation and data collection. Linux emerged as a viable candidate because of its ability to thrive in distributed computing networks and its support from a global community of developers constantly improving its performance and processes.

Today, with missions targeting not only Mars but also potential expeditions to asteroids and moons, the role of the operating system has never been more critical. It is essential to develop systems that can withstand cosmic radiation, manage energy efficiently, and perform real-time processing to respond to unforeseen events. The demands placed on modern spacecraft require an operating system that is not only resilient but also scalable and interoperable with other systems.

Historical insights into the evolution of operating systems in space provide crucial perspectives as we prepare Linux for its role in future Martian missions. By understanding the lessons learned and recognizing the milestones achieved in the past, we can better tailor and optimize Linux as a cohesive part of our exploration toolkit. This comprehensive understanding not only guides the technical specifications we aim for in underpinning next-generation systems but also informs the cultural practices that will govern how we collaborate and innovate in this ultimate frontier. As researchers and engineers build upon this rich historical context, they set the stage for the next chapter of human exploration, where robust operating systems are indispensable in our quest to unveil the mysteries of the cosmos.

2.2. The Demands of Outer Space on Technology

The journey into outer space presents unique and multifaceted demands on technology that dictate how systems are designed, implemented, and maintained. Operating within the frictionless vacuum of space introduces challenges that terrestrial technology seldom encounters. Engineers and developers must address these challenges within the context of space exploration by creating solutions that can withstand not only the harsh environmental conditions but also the unique operational requirements of off-Earth missions.

One of the first and foremost challenges is the extreme temperature fluctuations experienced in space. Equipment must function within a temperature range that can vary significantly, from the blistering heat of direct sunlight to the frigid cold of the shadowed regions of celestial bodies. This necessitates the development of specialized thermal control systems that can protect sensitive electronics. These systems may involve advanced materials with high thermal resistivity and innovative heat dissipation techniques, enabling technology to remain operational despite outer space's harsh climate.

Radiation exposure is another critical consideration. Space technology must be designed to withstand cosmic radiation and solar energetic particle events that can disrupt electronics and compromise the integrity of data. The strategies employed to mitigate these risks include using radiation-hardened components, shielding materials, and creating redundant systems that ensure continued operation in the event of radiation-related failures. Additionally, an operating system deployed in outer space must be capable of detecting when components are nearing their failure thresholds due to radiation damage, allowing for proactive remediation.

The lack of continuous connectivity poses another challenge. Unlike Earth, where reliable and instantaneous connections facilitate constant updates and support from central servers, space operations often depend on time-delayed communications. The time it takes for signals to traverse the vast distance between Earth and Mars can be anywhere from 4 to 24 minutes, introducing latency that complicates real-time operations. For example, autonomous robotic systems must be able to perform effectively without the benefit of real-time guidance from Earth-based operators. Consequently, the developers of space-exploration technology must ensure that systems are capable of significant autonomy, guided by robust artificial intelligence algorithms and efficient processing capabilities.

Additionally, the need for extended operational lifespans for space missions drives the demand for resilience in technology. Systems need to be capable of functioning for many years under extreme conditions with minimal maintenance. This requires not just durable materials and components but also a software architecture that can support long-term operations. For instance, applications running on the Linux operating system can be engineered for efficiency, security, and flexibility, facilitating updates and modifications as necessary over the years to adapt to unforeseen challenges.

The integration of automation and artificial intelligence (AI) into space systems introduces another layer of complexity. Although AI has gained considerable traction in terrestrial applications, its deployment in space technology introduces unique demands. Systems must be designed to react autonomously, making real-time decisions based on sensory data without waiting for directives from mission control. This capability is critical for navigating unknown terrain, conducting scientific experiments, and managing day-to-day operations. The algorithms employed must be efficient in both computation and energy usage, given that resources like power are often limited on off-Earth missions.

Critical to successful space missions, including those on Mars, is the scalability of technology. Systems must be built with modular designs to allow for easy upgrades or reconfiguration as missions evolve. For instance, a rover equipped with Linux can have different software components deployed based on mission requirements, whether for exploration, data collection, or sample analysis. This modularity extends to hardware as well, as systems may need to be adapted or expanded to accommodate new instruments or capabilities over time.

Another underappreciated aspect of space technology's demands is its reliance on rigorous testing protocols. Before any system is sent into space, extensive testing must be conducted to simulate the conditions of outer space. This often includes thermal vacuum tests, vibration tests, and radiation exposure assessments. Running Linux within these simulations allows developers to gather comprehensive data on system performance and make necessary adjustments, providing vital insights before actual deployment.

Finally, the operational ecosystem defined by collaborative international efforts adds complexity to technological demands. With various teams and organizations often working together on missions, interoperability between systems becomes paramount. Linux, with its open-source nature, provides a foundation for creating collaborative platforms that are easily modifiable and shareable among varied international partners. Through shared development initiatives, teams can leverage collaboration, pooling resources and knowledge to craft robust solutions that meet the distinct challenges of space exploration.

In conclusion, the demands of outer space on technology are vast and intricate. Engineers and developers face the formidable task of designing systems that not only operate efficiently but also adapt to the unpredictable nature of space environments. As we prepare for missions beyond Mars, it is clear that the operating systems at the command of these technologies, with Linux at the forefront, must rise to meet these formidable challenges, embodying resilience, adaptability, and ingenuity as we reach for the stars.

2.3. Linux: A Versatile Contender

Linux has distinguished itself as a versatile operating system suitable for the unique demands of space exploration, particularly for missions to Mars. Its open-source nature, extensive customization capabilities, and robust community support position it as a premier choice for the intricate and often unpredictable environments encountered beyond Earth's atmosphere. A thorough examination reveals several key characteristics that render Linux a formidable contender in the context of Martian missions and more broadly in extraterrestrial operations.

To begin with, the open-source architecture of Linux allows for unparalleled flexibility and adaptability. When dealing with the unknowns of Martian exploration, requirements can rapidly evolve as new challenges arise. Linux's open-source model enables engineers and developers to modify the operating system to meet specific mission needs. This adaptability is critical for space missions that often need to incorporate new tools and functionalities in response to dynamic environmental conditions or changing mission parameters. Unlike proprietary systems, where all changes must go through a commercial entity, Linux empowers teams to iterate on existing systems quickly, allowing for timely adjustments without the lengthy approval processes inherent in closed-source software.

Additionally, Linux is renowned for its modular structure. This modularity facilitates the creation of tailored distributions—specific versions of Linux designed to address particular functionalities relevant to a mission's goals. Whether it is managing robotics, controlling scientific instruments, or conducting data analysis, different Linux distributions can be developed to optimize performance for each task. For example, a modified Linux distribution could be designed to operate specialized cameras for geological surveys of the Martian surface, while another could efficiently manage power resources for sustained operations in the challenging Martian climate. The combination of modularity and customization ensures that systems can be developed with precision targeting their unique operational requirements.

Furthermore, the versatility of Linux extends to the advancements in real-time processing capabilities—a necessity for modern space missions. As spacecraft and rovers operate in environments where latency could potentially jeopardize mission success, the capacity for real-time data processing becomes increasingly vital. Linux supports a variety of real-time extensions, enabling developers to create applications that react swiftly to sensor inputs and environmental changes. This capability is particularly pertinent in autonomous systems, where rovers need to navigate rugged terrains without direct human intervention. Linux-based systems can be engineered to process vast amounts of information on-the-fly, utilizing advanced algorithms to make navigational decisions based on real-time data, enhancing the agility and effectiveness of automated operations.

Moreover, Linux's commitment to stability and reliability reinforces its suitability for long-duration missions. The unique pressure of maintaining systems over extended periods, often with limited opportunities for maintenance, demands an operating system that is not only secure but resilient to potential errors. Linux has earned a reputation for its stability and proven track record in mission-critical environments. The existence of extensive user documentation and a vibrant community further amplifies Linux's strengths, as developers can readily access shared knowledge and solutions, facilitating rapid troubleshooting and system optimization. This collective intelligence translates into a formidable support system that can rapidly respond to unforeseen issues encountered in the field.

Another important aspect of Linux's versatility is its compatibility with various hardware architectures. Given the diversity of devices employed in interplanetary exploration—from high-powered servers housed in spacecraft to compact, energy-efficient systems deployed on rovers—Linux's ability to run on a multitude of platforms makes it an attractive solution. This compatibility allows for coherent operation across various hardware, which can simplify integration, maintenance, and upgrades while ensuring consistent performance across different mission components.

Security is also a prominent consideration in any application of Linux within space exploration. As interplanetary missions venture into uncharted territories, ensuring the integrity and confidentiality of data becomes paramount. The open-source nature of Linux allows for continuous scrutiny by global developers, fostering a culture of proactive security monitoring and improvement. This community-driven approach ensures vulnerabilities can be identified and mitigated more efficiently, reducing risks associated with cyber threats that could potentially compromise mission success.

Notably, the scalability of Linux cannot be overlooked. The exponential growth of technology means that future missions to Mars or beyond may leverage computational capabilities that we can scarcely envision today. Linux supports the implementation of distributed computing models, allowing data processing tasks to be distributed across multiple devices or nodes. This capability not only enhances computational efficiency but also facilitates the optimization of resource management, critical for sustaining long-term missions in environments like Mars.

Another key strength of Linux is its ability to support collaborative developments on an international scale. As space exploration continues to be a collaborative effort among various countries and organizations, the open nature of Linux allows for the sharing of software components, tools, and best practices. Teams can contribute to a shared library of code, enhancing innovation and reinforcing community contributions that align with the needs of diverse missions. This engagement not only decentralizes development efforts but enriches Linux's capabilities, as contributions from a global pool of talent can help refine systems tailored for the stark realities of Martian exploration.

Finally, the evolving landscape of artificial intelligence and machine learning applications further illustrates the relevance of Linux in the context of modern space missions. The robustness of the Linux operating system provides an ideal platform for implementing complex AI algorithms, enabling adaptive systems that can learn from their environment and improve performance over time. Incorporating AI capabilities can empower rovers and other autonomous systems to analyze data, navigate obstacles, and even predict equipment failures, facilitating a more proactive approach to operational challenges.

In summation, Linux's flexibility, modularity, and reliability position it as a leading candidate for supporting the technological backbone of Martian exploration. As we look toward ambitious missions to the Red Planet and beyond, the versatility of Linux stands out, capable of responding to the demands of an unpredictable and extreme environment while fostering innovation and collaboration across international boundaries. Its established track record in real-time processing, adaptability to diverse hardware, and robust community support create a foundation upon which reliable systems for interplanetary exploration can be built, signaling a promising future for Linux in the cosmos.

2.4. Customizations for Space Deployment

In preparing Linux for deployment in space, particularly for Martian exploration, several critical customizations and adaptations are essential to ensure the operating system can function effectively in the unique and challenging environment of space. This process involves tailoring the OS to meet the harsh realities of Martian conditions while maximizing its capabilities to support mission objectives. Given the unpredictable nature of space operations and the need for reliability, these customizations must be executed with forethought and precision.

One primary area of focus is the design of a lightweight Linux kernel optimized for performance and resource management. Given the limited computational resources onboard space vehicles, developers need to ensure that the operating system runs efficiently without consuming excessive memory or processing power. Many space missions involve compact hardware with constrained processing capabilities, necessitating a minimalist kernel without unnecessary components that could lead to inefficiencies. Engineers can achieve this by stripping down the kernel to its essential modules, ensuring only the necessary drivers and functionalities are included. This not only enhances performance but also reduces the chances of software failure as fewer components mean fewer points of potential conflict.

Furthermore, hardening the OS against environmental pressures is crucial. Spacecraft operating in the Martian atmosphere are subjected to drastic temperature swings, radiation exposure, and dust accumulation. Software configurations should reflect this by implementing robust monitoring systems that can detect hardware anomalies signaling possible component failure. Additionally, creating a fault-tolerant system is essential to ensure that the software can gracefully handle errors or disruptions. For instance, Linux can be customized to support automated recovery protocols, allowing systems to either reboot certain services or switch to backup components without operator intervention. This capability is paramount in a scenario where communication with Earth might be delayed or interrupted.

Another fundamental aspect lies in the autonomy and decision-making capabilities of Linux. Given the significant communication delays involved in Earth-Mars communications, systems deployed on Mars must be equipped to operate autonomously, making real-time decisions based on situational data. Developers can customize Linux to include advanced artificial intelligence modules that allow rover systems to process inputs from various sensors and cameras, enabling them to navigate and adjust operations without awaiting instructions from mission control. Implementing such a closed-loop system bolsters mission success rates and minimizes risks associated with operational latency.

To further enhance adaptability in Martian conditions, Linux can be equipped with real-time operating system (RTOS) functionalities. The integration of real-time processing capabilities allows developers to allocate computational resources to critical tasks—prioritizing immediate responses or adjustments without delays. Such real-time capabilities are essential for systems managing multiple simultaneous inputs, such as navigation, scientific experiments, and maintenance operations. Customizing Linux in this manner prepares it to handle the intricacies of Martian exploration effectively.

For hardware compatibility, the custom-built Linux distributions must ensure seamless operation across different platforms, particularly as the diversity of devices may vary from landers and rovers to habitats and scientific equipment. Designing hardware abstraction layers compatible with the targeted devices enables the software to interact with various hardware components uniformly. This not only simplifies development and maintenance but also enhances the overall integration of systems within multivehicle operations, permitting harmonized functionality across the mission.

As energy management is a vital consideration for sustainable operations on Mars, specifically custom power management tools for Linux to monitor energy consumption and optimize power distribution add significant value. Custom scripts and daemons can be crafted to assess the power requirements of different tasks versus the current available resources, allowing for intelligent switching between high-power and low-power states. Such energy-conscious approaches ensure that limited resources are used judiciously over an extended mission timeline.

In the context of cybersecurity, customizing Linux involves implementing advanced security measures tailored for the vulnerabilities of space operations. With systems communicating across long distances and potentially coming under threat from rogue signals or malicious entities, configurations should include robust encryption protocols securing all data pipelines. Moreover, establishing security policies that continuously monitor for anomalies serves as a defensive measure against potential breaches that could disrupt missions.

Testing and validation are crucial phases of customization. Before deployment, all configured systems must be subjected to rigorous testing to verify their resilience against Martian conditions. This includes running simulations that replicate temperature extremes, radiation exposure, and operational scenarios mimicking anticipated missions. Utilizing test environments, engineers can collect performance data, identify potential flaws, and iteratively refine the software ahead of actual deployment.

In essence, the customizations required for Linux to thrive in space deployment revolve around optimizing performance for constrained resources, enhancing safety and reliability, and ensuring systems can autonomously handle the challenges posed by the Martian environment. These comprehensive modifications pave the way for a successful operating framework that enables diverse applications on Mars, ultimately contributing to the larger goals of sustaining exploration efforts and paving the way for human presence on the Red Planet. Through these innovations and adaptations, Linux not only shows its versatility but also stands as a resilient backbone for the future of space exploration.

2.5. Case Studies of Linux in Previous Missions

In examining the role and impact of Linux in past space missions, particularly the International Space Station (ISS), we uncover rich case studies that illuminate the operating system's transformative potential in demanding environments. The ISS, a multinational collaborative project, serves as a prime example of Linux's adaptability, resilience, and usability in the unforgiving realm of outer space.

Launched in 1998, the ISS has become a laboratory for scientific research and technological advancements, supporting a wide array of experiments and operations conducted by astronauts from various nations. Early on, NASA recognized the need for a flexible and robust operating system to manage the multitude of systems onboard the station. In light of this necessity, Linux was integrated into its operational framework due to its open-source nature, customizability, and strong community support. The ISS's implementation of Linux demonstrates various dimensions of how this operating system can be adapted and employed effectively in space missions.

One notable project utilizing Linux on the ISS is the Computer on the ISS (COTS) initiative. COTS aimed to utilize commercial off-the-shelf technology to reduce costs while still ensuring high reliability. Linux was selected to power these systems due to its proven stability and performance. This deployment allowed engineers to leverage existing innovations while maintaining the flexibility to develop and modify software as requirements evolved. As new capabilities were added, the ISS benefited from a collaborative environment where engineers could customize Linux to integrate advanced instrumentation and automation systems, thereby enhancing research capabilities in microgravity.

Furthermore, the ability to emit and process vast amounts of data is paramount on the ISS, where researchers conduct experiments ranging from fluid dynamics and combustion to fundamental physics and biology. Data management systems running on Linux enabled seamless data acquisition and real-time processing, empowering astronauts to communicate results back to Earth efficiently. The software developed around the Linux ecosystem allows the ISS crew to manipulate experiments, gather insights, and manage resources dynamically, fostering a culture of innovation and adaptability. In this context, the deployment of Linux was crucial; it facilitated the integration of robust scientific tools while accommodating the unique operational needs of space research.

Another compelling case study is the Linux-based deployment of robotic systems on the ISS. For instance, the Canadian Space Agency's Canadarm2, a robotic system used for assembly and maintenance tasks, operates with systems running on Linux. The inclusion of Linux for controlling robotic arms showcases its real-time processing capabilities and responsiveness needed to execute precision tasks within the station. Utilizing Linux not only streamlined the programming of these robots but also enabled engineers to easily update software configurations for enhanced functionalities in response to the ever-changing needs of ongoing ISS missions.

Security has become increasingly important as more systems on the ISS rely on interconnected technologies. Linux provides a rich security paradigm rooted in community collaboration, allowing for proactive updates and security measures that protect data integrity. The openness of Linux invites rigorous scrutiny by a global developer community, which can identify vulnerabilities and roll out fixes rapidly. On the ISS, this collaborative security approach offers a degree of resilience against potential threats, ensuring that critical data and systems remain operational while safeguarding sensitive information transmitted between crew members and mission control on Earth.

The evolution of the ISS and its various technological systems has also been significantly influenced by the core principles of open-source development. The architecture of Linux fosters a culture of shared knowledge, where developers from multiple nations can contribute to advancing spacecraft technologies. This collaborative ethos not only streamlines development practices but amplifies the contributions of a diverse pool of talent in pushing forward various (and often competing) research agendas. As various groups work on their Linux-inspired systems, the result is a rich and diverse landscape of software innovations that benefit all space agencies involved in the ISS.

Beyond just the ISS, Linux has found a place in other missions that utilized Linux for specialized roles. For example, the Linux operating system has been deployed on various rovers, such as the Mars rovers

Spirit and Opportunity. These rovers facilitated the exploration of Martian terrain and the analysis of geological features while employing customized Linux distributions adapted to the constraints posed by the Martian environment.

Taking a broader view, the success of Linux in these applications speaks to a fundamental shift in how space agencies approach mission-critical software development. With the pressing need for rapid iterations, open-source frameworks allow agencies to implement features and benefits quickly, accommodate the constant evolution of technology, and deploy systems integrated copiously.

Furthermore, as plans for future exploration, including missions to Mars and beyond, gain momentum, lessons drawn from the ISS's case studies emphasize the importance of continuous improvement, modular adaptability, and community collaboration. These tenets not only serve to enhance software development for individual missions but also contribute to the collective advancement of humanity's ventures into space.

In summary, the case studies of Linux in previous missions, particularly on the ISS, highlight its effectiveness as a reliable operating system in demanding conditions. This historical overview underscores its open-source flexibility, robust community engagement, and suitability for various mission-critical functions. As we prepare for the next generational leap in space exploration, the insights gained from these case studies will be instrumental in shaping the development and deployment strategies of Linux-based systems on Mars and in other potential lunar ventures. Embracing these lessons will ensure that Linux continues to serve as a linchpin in the transformative evolution of space exploration technology, fostering innovation and facilitating humanity's ambitions in the cosmos.

3. Understanding the Basics of Linux

3.1. Kernel Structure and Functionality

The Linux kernel represents the core of the operating system, serving as a critical intermediary between the hardware and software layers of any Linux-based system. Understanding its structure and functionality is vital for tailoring Linux for use in extreme environments such as Mars, where the demands on technology are exceptional and the stakes are high.

At its essence, the Linux kernel is responsible for managing system resources and enabling communication between software applications and hardware components. It is designed with a modular architecture, allowing for the inclusion of only the necessary components needed for specific tasks, which is particularly advantageous in constrained environments like space missions. The kernel operates in two primary modes: user mode and kernel mode. User mode is where applications operate with restricted access to system resources, ensuring that errors in user programs do not compromise the whole system. In contrast, kernel mode provides complete control over the system hardware, allowing the kernel to manage resources effectively.

One significant aspect of the kernel's functionality is its process management capabilities. The kernel is responsible for scheduling processes, managing their execution, and ensuring that they have access to CPU time when required. This involves allocating resources dynamically, which is crucial for space missions where multiple tasks must often be executed simultaneously, such as data collection from instruments, navigation adjustments, and communication with Earth-based command centers. The kernel's scheduling algorithms can be optimized to prioritize time-sensitive tasks, ensuring that critical functions are executed in real-time, particularly for autonomous operations in unpredictable environments.

Memory management is another critical function of the kernel. It oversees the allocation and deallocation of memory to processes, ensuring that memory leaks do not occur and that the available memory is optimally used. The kernel employs virtual memory techniques, allowing systems to appear as though they have more memory than is physically available. This is particularly beneficial for missions with hardware limitations, as it allows for more efficient use of resources. Given Mars' harsh conditions, excessive resource consumption might lead to system failure, so optimizing memory management through the kernel is imperative.

Device drivers are an integral part of the kernel structure, enabling communication between the operating system and peripheral hardware components. Linux supports a vast assortment of device drivers, making it incredibly adaptable to different hardware configurations. This flexibility is essential for missions that may need to integrate various sensors, cameras, and communication devices specific to Mars exploration. Customizing the kernel to utilize only necessary drivers ensures that systems can run efficiently while conserving power— an essential consideration for long-duration missions where energy resources may be severely limited.

Another critical component is the file system management handled by the kernel. It organizes data storage and retrieval, ensuring that files are saved and accessed efficiently. In the context of Mars missions, where vast amounts of data will be generated from scientific experiments, Rover imagery, and environmental monitoring, effective file system management becomes crucial. The kernel's ability to support different file systems means that engineers can choose the most suitable option for their data management needs, whether it be ext3, ext4, or others designed for specific purposes. This capability allows mission planners to optimize how data is stored and accessed, facilitating quick retrieval for analysis and transmission back to Earth.

Linux kernels are also built with security features that are critical for space missions. The kernel provides mechanisms for user authentication, access control, and secure communication, which are essential for safeguarding sensitive mission data and command protocols from potential threats. Specifically, areas exposed to public access can be secured to prevent unauthorized access, ensuring that mission-critical data remains protected in the face of vulnerabilities that could arise from the space environment.

The Linux kernel's networking capabilities also play a pivotal role in operations on Mars. The kernel supports various networking protocols, including TCP/IP, which are essential for communication between rovers, landers, and Earth. Given the expected communication delays and disruptions that can occur due to the vast distances between planets, having a reliable and configurable networking stack within the Linux kernel will significantly enhance the ability for mission control to receive data and send commands effectively. Customizing these networking functions to account for the specific characteristics of interplanetary communication will enable the system to manage connectivity efficiently and ensure robust data transmission.

Moreover, the kernel's real-time capabilities can be enabled through specific extensions, responding to the need for operating systems to process information and react without delay, which is crucial in the autonomous navigation of rovers and drones. Such real-time extensions enable interrupts to be handled with minimal latency, ensuring that mission-critical decisions can be made on the fly based on immediate observations from the Martian environment.

As we continually evolve the kernel to meet the specific challenges of Mars exploration, modifications could allow engineers to introduce additional functionalities such as enhanced telemetry for monitoring system health, improved logging for capturing environmental data, and fault-tolerant mechanisms to ensure continuous operation in the event of hardware failures. Such advancements are essential for enabling sustained human and robotic exploration of the Red Planet.

In conclusion, understanding the structure and functionality of the Linux kernel is paramount for deploying effective solutions in the demanding context of Martian exploration. The kernel's design allows it to manage resources flexibly and efficiently while maintaining security and reliability in operations. By optimizing and customizing the kernel to meet the specific needs of space missions, we can ensure that Linux functions at its best when faced with the unique challenges presented by the Martian environment, paving the way for successful exploration and research activities on our nearest planetary neighbor.

3.2. Linux Distributions Overview

Linux distributions are a key element in understanding how this versatile operating system can be tailored to meet the unique challenges posed by missions to Mars and other space exploration ventures. Distinct from a single operating system, a distribution encompasses the core Linux kernel along with a collection of software and applications that fit specific end-user requirements. This flexibility, combined with the broad spectrum of available distributions, allows developers and engineers to customize Linux for the specific needs of interplanetary operations.

To start, it is essential to recognize the diversity that exists within the Linux ecosystem. There are numerous distributions available, each with its unique characteristics, system requirements, and targeted use cases. Some of the most renowned distributions include Ubuntu, Fedora, CentOS, Debian, and Arch Linux, among others. Each of these distributions serves different purposes, from general-purpose computing to specialized applications in scientific research, server operation, or embedded systems.

For space missions, particularly those aiming for Mars, the focus usually shifts toward distributions that prioritize stability, performance, and low resource consumption. Scientific Linux, for example, was designed as a distribution for high-performance scientific computing and serves as an excellent choice for tasks requiring extensive computational power and reliability. Its structure supports a robust environment for running complex simulations and processing large datasets—an essential factor when analyzing Mars' geology or atmospheric conditions.

Another notable example is the Debian distribution, known for its strong emphasis on stability and security. Debian's long-standing reputation within the Linux community makes it a strong candidate for use in applications where reliability is paramount. Spacecraft onboard systems often need to operate for extended periods with minimal maintenance; thus, deploying an operating system based on Debian could provide the advantages of reliability and a well-maintained code base. Furthermore, it also allows for a significant level of customization, enabling developers to strip unnecessary components or integrate specific applications designed for Martian exploration.

One cannot overlook the role of real-time distributions for managing the immediacy of tasks required in space operations. Real-time Linux distributions, which are configured to process data inputs and execute instructions with minimal latency, allow spacecraft systems to respond promptly to environmental changes. For instance, the Xenomai real-time framework offers capabilities critical for robotic systems on Mars that require high levels of responsiveness when navigating the diverse and often unpredictable Martian terrain.

In addition to individual distributions, the concept of lightweight adaptations of these operating systems cannot be underestimated. Lightweight distributions such as Alpine Linux or Puppy Linux can be especially valuable in space missions, where hardware constraints are a constant concern. These distributions require fewer system resources, thus allowing the onboard systems to run smoothly without burdening the limited processing and memory capabilities available on spacecraft or rovers. Those lightweight systems can help extend the operational lifespan of spacecraft software by conserving memory and processing power, essential commodities in Martian environments.

Another important facet of Linux distributions is the ability to create custom spins or specialized versions tailored to specific hardware or operational requirements—an aspect particularly advantageous in the context of space missions. By creating a custom Linux distribution specifically designed for a mission—one that includes only the necessary applications, performance tweaks, and drivers—mission planners can ensure that the OS runs optimally on the available hardware while also anticipating the unique challenges encountered during operations on Mars.

The open-source nature of Linux distributions also fosters collaboration and innovation, which is a vital aspect of the development process for space exploration technology. An open approach allows developers across various space agencies and companies to contribute to enhancements, bug fixes, and new features. This communal effort results in continuous improvement of the distributions over time, which can be quickly adapted to meet new challenges or requirements as they arise.

Furthermore, integrating supporting applications that align with scientific research is another identity marker of specific Linux distributions that strike a chord with space missions. Many Linux-based applications, such as Metacity for handling graphical interfaces or Gnuplot for scientific graphing, seamlessly operate within the Linux ecosystem, removing the need to seek separate solutions for tasks related to data visualization or remote operation management.

Moreover, a focus must also be placed on security—a vital consideration for any operating system that will be deployed in unpredictable environments like Mars. Different Linux distributions come with varying security features out of the box and can enhance or configure security protocols according to mission requirements. Such adaptations might involve customizing firewall settings, setting up secure SSH access for remote management, or ensuring all data transmissions are encrypted using secure protocols.

Finally, as we consider the far-reaching aspirations of future space exploration missions beyond Mars, the adaptability of Linux distributions to work with emerging technologies must also be factored in. As newer communication technologies, advanced robotics, and AI systems are developed, Linux distributions must evolve to integrate those advancements seamlessly.

In conclusion, the overview of Linux distributions highlights their adaptability and customized nature, making them suited for the ever-evolving needs of space exploration. As we chart a course for missions to Mars, the selection, customization, and optimization of Linux distributions will become increasingly pivotal in preparing our technology to succeed in the harsh conditions of the Red Planet, ensuring that we are not only equipped for the challenges we face but also ready to innovate and adapt in real-time. The Linux ecosystem stands as a robust foundation on which the future of interplanetary technology can be built, giving us the tools we need to explore the cosmos with confidence.

3.3. Open-Source Community and Development

In the realm of technology and software development, the ethos of open-source communities stands at the forefront of innovation, collaboration, and adaptability. This is especially pertinent when considering the application and evolution of Linux, which has become synonymous with flexibility and community-driven advancement—a crucial factor as we prepare for ambitious missions to Mars.

Open-source community and development embody the idea that software can thrive when shared, built upon, and collaboratively enhanced. The Linux operating system, initiated by Linus Torvalds in the early 1990s, emerged from this ideal, inviting anyone interested to contribute to its evolution. This engaging model fosters an environment where developers from varied backgrounds unite to address complex challenges, share diverse ideas, and fortify a thriving ecosystem that can pivot and adapt in response to new demands, including those posed by space exploration missions.

As the dawn of interplanetary exploration approaches, the open-source community around Linux presents a vital resource for engineers and developers tasked with preparing robust systems for Mars. One enlightening aspect of this community is its collective intelligence—a hallmark of open-source projects that allows programmers from disparate corners of the globe to pool resources, share knowledge, and troubleshoot issues. This ingenuity proves essential for interplanetary missions, as the collaborative spirit nurtured by open-source can rapidly address complexities inherent in hostile environments, such as the challenges posed by dust storms, cosmic radiation, and unknown terrain on the Martian surface.

The participation in the open-source community extends beyond merely writing code; it encompasses the principles of continuous integration and rapid iteration. Engineers on projects aimed at Martian exploration can leverage existing codebases, avoiding redundancies while enhancing functionality. By allowing developers to build on the work of their peers, Linux's open-source model enables the community to shift gears, quickly developing adaptations or patches needed for unique mission requirements. This means that when an unforeseen challenge emerges, such as a component failure or unexpected environmental condition, the responsiveness of the community can lead to timely software adjustments that enhance system resilience and avoid mission delays.

Linux's permeation into space technology can be observed through landmarks such as the European Space Agency's (ESA) Mars Express mission and NASA's Jet Propulsion Laboratory's (JPL) use of CGI and the open-source robotics operating system to facilitate the functioning of rovers and landers on Mars. In each of these instances, the flexibility of Linux, coupled with the collaborative efforts of the open-source community, manifested as a solid foundation for critical operations. The scientific community's ability to share code, algorithms, and instructions allows for rapid deployment of software updates and optimizations—critical factors when systems need to operate autonomously with limited human oversight.

Moreover, the open-source community contributes to the reliability and robustness of Linux as an operating system for space missions. Development stems from a variety of contributors, which means rigorous peer review of code becomes an integral part of the lifecycle of software improvement. In the landscape of space exploration, where the costs of failure are exorbitant and demand precision, this open and scrutinized approach to development instills a level of confidence that proprietary systems may lack. Many developers contribute to fixing bugs, enhancing security protocols, and optimizing performance—not just for their projects but for the greater good of all users, which is especially beneficial for applications deployed in unpredictable environments like Mars.

Simultaneously, the adaptability provided by Linux opens the door for new technologies and methods to integrate into existing frameworks seamlessly. Innovators within the community experiment and create applications tailored for specific instruments used in Martian missions—be it software for analyzing geological samples or frameworks for autonomous navigation systems. This adaptability empowers the gradual evolution of Linux distributions catering explicitly to the scientific requirements of interplanetary missions.

Additionally, the open-source community cultivates an inclusive culture that attracts diverse voices—each contributing unique insights to the development of systems designed for Mars. Engineers, scientists, and enthusiastic amateurs alike contribute to the advancement of the software, breaking down barriers, and collaborating across disciplinary lines. This pluralistic approach enriches the resulting technology, producing solutions that may not have emerged in more isolated programming environments.

Collaboration within the open-source community extends naturally to partnerships among international space agencies and private enterprises. As countries unite to explore the cosmos, they bring with them different sets of expectations, experiences, and technologies. A shared open-source framework, such as Linux, facilitates the pooling of efforts, allowing multiple agencies to leverage collective expertise and resources effectively. The significant advantage of this approach lies in the fact that any new findings, algorithms, or technologies developed are often shared across the global community, accelerating innovation and exploration.

Security too sees a substantial benefit from the contributions of the open-source community. With many eyes scrutinizing the software, vulnerabilities can be quickly identified and addressed before deployment, thus increasing the system's security profile—an essential factor for operating in environments where direct human intervention may not be possible for extended periods. Community-driven scripts and enhancements can also refine security metrics, ensuring Linux systems deployed on Mars stand resilient against potential threats.

In summary, the open-source community and its contributions to Linux development are invaluable as we prepare for the challenges of Mars exploration. By fostering collaboration, rapid adaptation, and continuous improvement, this community empowers engineers and developers to capitalize on the wealth of shared knowledge and resources, ultimately ensuring that Linux operates as a reliable and adaptable backbone for future missions beyond Earth. As we chart our course toward the Red Planet, the synergy between Linux and its open-source community illustrates a promising path forward—leading the way into the uncharted territories of space, knitting together innovation with exploration emphatically.

3.4. Security Features of Linux

Security features are paramount for the stability and integrity of any operating system, particularly one that is set to operate in the unforgiving environment of space. In the context of Mars exploration, Linux's security framework is designed not only to protect data and systems from external threats but also to ensure reliable operation amidst potential hardware compromises, environmental stressors, and the necessity for autonomous function. This deep dive into the security features of Linux aptly illustrates why it is particularly suitable for missions intending to push the boundaries of exploration.

At the core of Linux's security framework lies its permission model, which governs how users and processes interact with the system. By operating under a strict user privilege model, Linux minimizes the risk of unauthorized access to critical systems. Each file and process has associated permissions dictating who can read, modify, or execute it. This layered approach enables the operating system to compartmentalize functionalities effectively, reducing the attack surface an external threat can exploit. In the context of Mars, where human interaction may be limited, this is crucial for protecting systems from unauthorized commands that might otherwise disrupt mission objectives.

Kernel security modules are another critical component of Linux's robust security architecture. Tools such as SELinux (Security-Enhanced Linux) and AppArmor provide sophisticated access control mechanisms that further enhance the protection of onboard systems. They facilitate mandatory access controls (MAC) allowing stricter and fine-tuned policies governing system operations. For example, with SELinux, a system administrator can define policies that specify how processes interact with files. This degree of granularity is essential in a Martian setting, where a failure due to software misconfiguration or unverified access could have significant repercussions for the mission's success.

Given the potential for hardware vulnerabilities, particularly when equipment is subjected to extreme conditions, redundancy within systems becomes a fundamental security component. Linux supports multiple configurations for system redundancy, allowing for failover mechanisms that keep essential operations running in the event of a hardware failure. For Mars missions, this might involve having critical components running on redundant hardware, with the Linux OS capable of detecting a failure and automatically transferring processes to backup systems without human intervention. This level of reliability is crucial, ensuring that operations can continue seamlessly in the event of unpredicted failures, a significant risk factor in innovative environmental conditions.

Adapting to extreme environmental factors—such as high radiation and thermal swings—requires more than just hardware resilience; it also requires vigilant monitoring and logging systems. Linux distributions can be customized to employ detailed logging of system activities, enabling teams to track operations, identify anomalies, and respond quickly to incidents. Systems can be configured to proactively monitor vital metrics, generating alerts if conditions start trending outside of predefined thresholds. Effective logging not only helps in real-time monitoring but also aids in post-mission analysis, allowing engineers to review the operational conditions and security postures during space missions thoroughly.

Significant emphasis is also placed on data encryption features within Linux, providing a robust methodology for safeguarding mission-critical information from interception or unauthorized access. With encryption protocols implemented at different layers—from file-system encryption to secure communications protocols (like SSH) —data privacy is ensured in both transit and at rest. Given the communication delays and potential cybersecurity threats posed in interplanetary communication, employing encryption substantially mitigates the risks involved and assures that sensitive data remains confidential.

To reinforce its security architecture further, Linux benefits from its open-source nature, which fosters an environment of continuous scrutiny and improvement. The widespread developer community consistently monitors for vulnerabilities, and any identified issues are promptly addressed through updates and patches. This proactive approach means that as threats evolve, Linux can quickly adapt to mitigate risks, an essential aspect of ensuring cybersecurity on a mission to a volatile environment like Mars.

In addition to these foundational security features, Linux also supports various network security measures, including advanced firewall capabilities and intrusion detection systems (IDS). Specific configurations can restrict network access or log suspicious activities, enhancing the overall security infrastructure of the systems aboard Martian missions. Given the unpredictable nature of outer space, where communication networks will link to Earth, these measures bolster the integrity of data communications, reducing the chances of information compromise or sabotage.

Finally, fostering a culture of secure programming practices is critical when developing applications intended for use on Linux platforms in space. Educational programs may be implemented for developers involved in preparing Linux systems, promoting a rigorous understanding of security principles and challenges particular to space exploration. This cultural shift toward security-first development will enhance the robustness of applications built on Linux, ensuring they can withstand the rigors of Mars missions and operate reliably.

In summary, Linux's multifaceted security features position it as an ideal operating system for Martian exploration. By emphasizing access control, redundancy, real-time monitoring, encryption, community-driven improvement, and network security measures, Linux ensures resilience and reliability in the face of both external and internal threats. As we prepare for future missions beyond Earth, the robust security architecture of Linux equips us with the tools necessary to safeguard critical systems, paving the way for successful and secure explorations on the Red Planet and beyond.

3.5. Linux in Multi-Platform Environments

Linux stands out in multi-platform environments due to its inherent adaptability, modularity, and extensive support ecosystem. These attributes allow Linux to function effectively across a variety of hardware architectures, making it an ideal operating system for the diverse array of devices that may be deployed in Martian exploration contexts. From powerful landers equipped with sophisticated scientific instruments to nimble rovers tasked with traversing the Martian terrain, Linux can be tailored to meet the unique demands of each device, ensuring that all systems operate harmoniously within the larger mission framework.

One of the defining features of Linux is its open-source nature, allowing developers to create customized distributions that suit specific hardware configurations. For missions to Mars, engineers can craft lightweight, specialized versions of Linux tailored for the resource-constrained environments of rovers or habitats. By stripping down unnecessary components and optimizing essential functionalities, these tailored distributions ensure that every bit of processing power and memory is utilized efficiently. This modularity enables developers to select only the needed drivers and applications pertinent to the mission's goals, significantly enhancing performance and reliability.

Linux's compatibility spans a vast range of hardware architectures, including ARM, x86, and PowerPC. This flexibility is particularly significant in multi-platform environments, where different devices may rely on distinct kinds of processors or system configurations. For instance, a rover may incorporate an ARM-based processor for energy efficiency, while a lander could utilize an x86-based architecture for robust computational capacity. By providing support for multiple architectures, Linux facilitates seamless integration among these components, ensuring that cross-communication between devices occurs effortlessly.

Another vital aspect of Linux in multi-platform scenarios is its comprehensive driver support. The Linux kernel is equipped with a vast library of device drivers, which enables it to interface with an extensive variety of hardware peripherals. In the context of space exploration, where new and specialized devices are often developed, the ability of Linux to incorporate new drivers is essential. Whether integrating novel sensors for environmental monitoring or advanced cameras for geological analysis, Linux can adapt to these requirements, ensuring compatibility and functionality.

Moreover, the multi-platform capabilities of Linux extend beyond hardware configurations to include diverse networking environments. In space missions, establishing reliable communication between devices is vital for operational success. The Linux networking stack supports various protocols and configurations that facilitate inter-device communication, allowing rovers, landers, and other systems to exchange data reliably. This feature is particularly important on Mars, where real-time data exchange is necessary for autonomous systems to collaborate effectively. By leveraging robust networking capabilities, Linux ensures that devices can operate as a cohesive unit, conducting complex tasks efficiently.

In addition to hardware adaptability and driver support, the open-source nature of Linux fosters collaboration among developers worldwide. As more space agencies and private enterprises engage in Martian exploration, the ability to share code, libraries, and tools becomes increasingly valuable. The collaborative ethos inherent in the Linux community allows different teams to build upon one another's work, ultimately leading to the rapid development of innovative solutions that can be applied across various platforms. This cross-pollination of ideas not only accelerates technological advancements but also solidifies Linux's status as a versatile operating environment capable of addressing complex challenges.

Another critical consideration is the need for resilience in multi-platform environments, especially in the harsh conditions encountered on Mars. Linux provides a robust framework for system redundancy and failover mechanisms, which can be implemented across different platforms. If one device experiences failure, others can assume critical functions, ensuring continuous operation. Such resilience is crucial for space missions, where human intervention may be limited due to communication delays. Implementing these features on Linux-based systems guarantees that essential functions remain operational, promoting mission success and reliability.

The ability to operate in heterogeneous environments enables Linux to support a range of applications that span scientific research, data analysis, and autonomous navigation. Within a Martian mission, different devices may be tasked with specific roles, from collecting and analyzing mineral samples to mapping the terrain using advanced sensors. The flexibility of Linux allows developers to create specialized applications for each device while ensuring that applications can communicate and work together as part of a larger mission strategy.

In summary, the adaptability of Linux across various hardware platforms is not merely an advantage, but a necessity for Martian exploration missions. Its open-source nature, extensive driver support, modular architecture, and robust networking capabilities enable Linux to operate seamlessly across a diverse array of devices. This adaptability is further enhanced by the collaborative spirit of the Linux community, which collectively drives innovations that contribute to the success of space missions. As we prepare to traverse the challenges of Mars, leveraging Linux's multi-platform capabilities will undoubtedly become a cornerstone of our exploration strategy, ensuring that we are equipped to face the complexities of the final frontier with confidence.

4. Mars: The Final Frontier for Technology

4.1. Understanding Martian Conditions

The Martian environment is a formidable and varied landscape that presents numerous challenges, necessitating a deep understanding of its conditions for successful exploration and habitation. Delving into the Martian atmosphere, temperature variations, dust storms, radiation levels, and the planet's geological characteristics reveals the complexity of preparing technology for deployment in such a harsh setting.

Mars presents a thin atmosphere composed primarily of carbon dioxide (about 95%), making it significantly less dense than Earth's atmosphere, which presents considerable challenges for maintaining human life and operating machinery. The atmospheric pressure on Mars is less than 1% of Earth's, equivalent to being at an altitude of around 30 kilometers on Earth. This low pressure creates a hostile environment where any equipment or habitats must be tightly sealed to avoid decompression and the escape of atmospheric gases, as well as to prevent the ingress of harmful dust particles that might compromise systems and payloads.

Temperature extremes on Mars are both intense and variable. While daytime temperatures near the equator may reach as high as 20 degrees Celsius (68 degrees Fahrenheit), nighttime temperatures can plunge to −73 degrees Celsius (-100 degrees Fahrenheit) or lower, particularly in the polar regions. These extreme fluctuations require robust thermal control systems for any technology deployed on Mars. Operating systems, especially, must be adapted to monitor and manage hardware temperatures to ensure that machinery functions reliably across a wide functionality range, preventing overheating during the warm Martian day and conserving power consumption during the frigid nights.

The prevalence of dust storms on Mars is another critical factor to consider. Dust storms can envelop vast areas of the planet, sometimes lasting for weeks or even months. These storms significantly reduce solar radiation, posing challenges for solar-powered equipment, and can also lead to abrasive wear on surfaces and mechanisms. Systems employed on Mars must be designed with protective measures against dust accumulation and triggered to perform maintenance routines when necessary. This includes the development of Linux-based applications that actively monitor environmental conditions and adjust systems accordingly to minimize exposure to this abrasive dust.

Radiation exposure on Mars is a serious concern due to its thin atmosphere and lack of a protective magnetic field. The radiation levels experienced on the Martian surface are about twice that of Earth and consist mainly of cosmic radiation, solar particle events, and secondary radiation resulting from interactions with the Martian surface. Prolonged exposure to this radiation can pose health risks to humans and lead to equipment malfunctions, particularly in sensitive electronic components. To mitigate radiation effects, Linux systems must incorporate checks that can monitor for radiation levels and adjust operations, such as powering down components during heightened exposure periods or employing radiation-hardened materials where practical.

The geology of Mars also plays a vital role in planning technological deployments. The Martian surface is a mix of volcanic rock, sedimentary features, and polar ice caps, suggesting that equipment may need to navigate varied terrain, which includes canyons, rust-colored regolith, and potential water-ice deposits beneath the surface. The operating systems need to adapt to gathering data from geological surveys, analyzing terrain features, and making real-time navigation decisions based on environmental inputs. Linux displays robust capabilities in managing complex data processing tasks, essential for the scientific analysis and navigation necessary to gather and interpret Martian geology efficiently.

The Martian conditions create a paradigm of challenges that greatly impact the design and operation of technology intended for exploration and potentially colonization. By understanding the specifics of atmospheric pressure, temperature fluctuations, dust storm phenomena, radiation exposure, and geological diversity, engineers and developers can strategically customize Linux and its affiliated systems to withstand the rigors of the Martian environment. Such in-depth knowledge not only enhances the reliability of technology but ultimately ensures mission success as we forge ahead into the cosmos, with Mars set as our next frontier.

4.2. Technological Needs for Survival on Mars

In the preparation for human survival on Mars, numerous technological needs emerge as crucial for both immediate survival and long-term habitation. Understanding these essential technologies is paramount for crafting a comprehensive strategy that ensures success in this demanding environment.

One of the foremost requirements is the establishment of life support systems capable of sustaining breathable air and potable water. Mars' atmosphere is predominantly carbon dioxide (approximately 95%), with only trace amounts of oxygen. Consequently, a reliable system must be developed to extract oxygen from the Martian regolith or generate it through chemical processes. Technologies for life support must also recycle carbon dioxide back into oxygen, similar to systems utilized aboard the International Space Station (ISS). For instance, engineers can employ technologies such as the Sabatier Process, which reacts carbon dioxide with hydrogen to produce methane and water —offering an effective way to generate oxygen through the reverse process. Customized Linux systems could manage these operations, ensuring that the balance of gases remains optimal for human needs.

Water generation and purification technologies are equally critical for survival. Research indicates that water ice lies beneath the surface of Mars in various locations, posing an opportunity for extraction. Technologies devised for melting, filtering, and recycling water must be robust and efficient. Advanced filtration systems to eliminate contaminants, integrated with automated monitoring and control systems powered by Linux, can ensure a continuous supply of clean water essential for hydration, agriculture, and sanitation.

Furthermore, food production technologies must be central to sustaining human life during long-term missions. Agricultural systems on Mars will need to integrate hydroponics or aeroponics techniques to grow food in a controlled environment. Using sensors and data analytics, Linux-based systems can monitor plant growth, nutrient levels, and conditions such as humidity and light. With adaptations for the peculiar Martian circumstances, including low gravity and extreme temperature variations, these systems can automate crop management, enhancing efficiency in food production.

Energy management is another crucial technological need. Mars' distance from the Sun means that solar energy must be harnessed effectively, while wind power could be considered, given Mars' windy conditions. Developing specialized solar panels optimized for Martian dust and temperature fluctuations is essential. Additionally, Linux systems would play a vital role in managing energy distribution, monitoring consumption, and controlling batteries to ensure continuous power supply for all operational needs.

Communication systems are imperative in supporting interaction between Mars and Earth. Given the distance, communication hiccups involving delays and interruptions may arise. Establishing a reliable data relay network through satellites in Martian orbit will facilitate steady communication lanes. Linux-based software can ensure efficient data routing, optimizing bandwidth utility, and providing redundancy in case of system failures. Furthermore, incorporating AI-driven algorithms for predictive analytics could enhance data handling capabilities, providing data compression and error-checking solutions tailored to the unique challenges of interplanetary communication.

Robotic and autonomous systems will be indispensable for aiding human efforts, particularly in hazardous environments. Rovers and drones can execute preliminary explorations, sample collections, and maintenance tasks. These systems must be equipped with sophisticated navigation and situational awareness capabilities. Linux's adaptability supports the deployment of AI algorithms for autonomous decision-making and machine learning applications that allow these systems to learn from their environment over time and optimize missions accordingly.

Materials used for constructing habitats and equipment must also be carefully considered. Technologies capable of producing building materials from in-situ resources—commonly referred to as in-situ resource utilization—will be essential to minimize transport costs from Earth. 3D printing technologies driven by Linux systems can fabricate structures using Martian soil and other local resources, reducing dependency on Earth-supplied materials.

Finally, health systems, including telemedicine technology, for health monitoring and emergency medical assistance become a priority. With long durations of isolation, fulfilling medical needs becomes vital. Incorporating remote diagnostic tools operated by Linux systems can enable astronauts to communicate health data to medical professionals on Earth, while onboard systems can support preventive healthcare measures tailored to the Martian environment.

In summary, the technological needs for survival on Mars are wide-ranging and interconnected, encompassing life support systems, energy management, food production, communication networks, robotic assistance, and health monitoring. Each of these components requires careful integration into a cohesive framework empowered by Linux, ensuring robustness, adaptability, and reliability in meeting the challenges posed by life on the Red Planet. As we advance towards these monumental missions, focusing on these essential technologies will be pivotal in laying the groundwork for a sustainable human presence on Mars.

4.3. Communication Systems on Mars

The communication systems on Mars are fundamental for the success of any mission, particularly as humanity aims for prolonged habitation and exploration of the Red Planet. Given the vast distances and the distinct challenges posed by the Martian environment, developing robust communication strategies between Earth and Mars is essential. Understanding the dynamics of communication, including the technological requirements, latency issues, network structure, and protocols, will set the stage for effective operations on Mars.

At the core of Mars communication is the establishment of an interplanetary network that ensures continuous connectivity between surface exploration assets and Earth. The most common method of communication has involved radio frequencies, which are capable of covering the immense distances between the two planets. These radio signals traverse through space at the speed of light, but the distances mean that communication can suffer from significant delays. For example, when Mars is at its closest point to Earth, the one-way communication latency is about 4 minutes, while at its furthest, it can reach up to 24 minutes. This inherent delay necessitates the need for autonomous operations in Martian missions, where systems must make real-time decisions without waiting for input from Earth.

To address these challenges, establishing a relay network of satellites in Martian orbit presents a promising solution. These satellites can facilitate continuous data transmission by receiving signals from Martian surface assets (like rovers) and relaying them back to Earth. NASA's Mars Reconnaissance Orbiter (MRO) and Mars Atmosphere and Volatile Evolution (MAVEN) are examples of satellites that operate in this capacity. By creating a robust infrastructure of orbiters, missions can reduce communication blind spots and increase the bandwidth available for data transfer, thereby improving the reliability of communication systems.

Moreover, optimizing data compression techniques is crucial given the limitations of bandwidth when sending information back to Earth. Communication from Mars may involve high-resolution images, scientific data, sensor readings, and command logs. Employing efficient data compression algorithms allows for maximizing the amount of information transmitted within the limited bandwidth, ensuring more valuable data can reach mission control. Linux-based systems can be programmed with advanced algorithms for data compression, enabling quicker and more efficient data transfers.

Security also plays an integral role in communication strategies for Martian missions. Given the potential risks of interception and unauthorized access, implementing robust encryption protocols is necessary to safeguard communications between Mars and Earth. Linux's user privilege models and open-source capabilities can be utilized to create complex security systems, ensuring that sensitive data remains confidential while in transit. This aspect of security can extend to the verification of incoming and outgoing communications, preventing any possible cyber threats that could compromise mission integrity.

Another significant challenge in Martian communications lies in the sustainability of communication technology. Devices must endure harsh conditions such as extreme temperatures, dust storms, and radiation exposure. The hardware used to facilitate communication must be both robust and efficient, often requiring radiation-hardened components to ensure their longevity. Customizing the Linux operating system for these devices involves optimizing drivers and applications to monitor real-time system performance and environmental conditions. Monitoring systems must be developed to autonomously assess hardware health, enabling prompt actions—such as recalibrating antennas or shutting down non-essential systems—whenever necessary.

Remote access and control must also be woven into the fabric of Martian communication systems. Engineers and scientists may wish to access data and control equipment remotely, necessitating a secure and reliable command and control infrastructure. Utilizing Linux-based systems, commands can be transmitted through satellite networks, ensuring that mission-critical operations can be executed seamlessly regardless of the distance. These systems should incorporate intelligent designs to manage communication queues effectively, allowing for operations to occur promptly even during periods of high latency.

Achieving real-time monitoring and data retrieval is vital in managing operations on Mars. By implementing a logging system with Linux that captures data from a range of instruments, scientists can analyze the information as it is collected. This approach can enhance the field of scientific discovery by allowing for live data visualization and assessment, with information being relayed back to mission control to inform decisions and strategy proactively.

Lastly, as the ambitions for Mars grow, so too must the communication framework adapt. Planning for long-term communications capability involves anticipating the evolution of technology and the potential establishment of human bases. Future communications may require the integration of advanced technologies such as laser communications or optical systems, which could transmit data at significantly higher speeds than current radio-wave systems. The adaptability of Linux would enable the implementation of new protocols needed to manage these advanced communication methods swiftly.

In conclusion, establishing effective communication systems on Mars is an intricate task that requires careful planning, technological innovation, and a robust framework to address the environmental challenges. By leveraging technologies such as satellite relay networks, data compression techniques, strong security protocols, and Linux-based applications, the journey toward sustainable and efficient communication on Mars can be realized. This communication backbone is not just about maintaining contact; it is central to the success of missions as we push the boundaries of human presence on the Red Planet. With a solid communication infrastructure, we lay the groundwork needed for exploration, research, and, ultimately, eventual colonization of Mars.

4.4. Energy Resources and Management

The exploration of energy resources on Mars is a multifaceted challenge that requires strategic planning and innovative approaches to ensure sustainable power supply for missions. Acknowledging the unique conditions present on Mars and tapping into renewable energy sources is crucial for both short-term expeditions and long-term habitation. The Martian environment presents distinct opportunities, notably in solar energy, wind energy, and the potential for in-situ resource utilization (ISRU), all of which can be harnessed effectively with the right technology and management systems powered by Linux.

Solar energy is often the first consideration when addressing energy needs on Mars, primarily because of the planet's relatively higher irradiance compared to Earth. Despite the thin atmosphere, Mars receives approximately 60% of the solar energy that Earth does. This provides an ample opportunity for solar panels to generate electricity. However, several factors must be considered, including the performance of solar panels under extreme temperature variations, dust accumulation, and reduced efficiency in the lower light conditions present during Martian winters.

To optimize solar energy capture, customized Linux systems can be deployed to manage solar arrays efficiently. This includes implementing tracking mechanisms that adjust the panels for maximum exposure to the sun's rays throughout the Martian day. Advanced energy management systems can continuously monitor performance and make real-time adjustments based on environmental conditions. For instance, applying algorithms that predict dust storms can enable the panels to reposition or activate self-cleaning mechanisms to ensure optimal energy collection.

In addition to solar energy, harnessing wind energy holds potential, especially during Martian dust storms, which are common and can result in sustained high winds. The thin atmosphere, however, poses challenges for traditional wind turbines since the power output is greatly influenced by air density. Researchers must investigate specialized turbine designs tailored for Martian conditions, where the focus could shift towards small, vertical-axis wind turbines that can operate efficiently despite lower wind speeds.

Energy resource management systems must be compatible with these diverse energy sources, requiring sophisticated software to allocate power according to mission needs. A Linux-based system can integrate multiple energy streams, facilitating smart grid technology that allows for a hybrid approach to power management. For example, during peak solar periods, excess energy can be stored in batteries or used to generate hydrogen through electrolysis, which can later be used as a fuel source for rover operations or other systems.

An essential aspect of managing these energy systems is the need for redundancy and reliability. Long-duration missions must ensure consistent energy availability. Linux systems can support robust architectures that account for potential failures in energy sources, implementing failover mechanisms that switch to alternative systems seamlessly. By employing advanced monitoring and predictive analytics, these systems can anticipate issues, allowing for proactive maintenance or adjustments to avoid outages.

Beyond renewable sources, in-situ resource utilization contributes significantly to sustainable energy management on Mars. Utilizing Martian resources to produce fuel – such as methane from the Sabatier reaction – can substantially lessen the need for Earth-supplied materials. This not only lowers costs but also extends mission capabilities. Linux-based control systems can manage the electrolysis and chemical processes involved, ensuring efficient conversion and storage of generated fuels.

Collaboration between energy resource management systems and autonomous AI operations is vital. Implementations of machine learning algorithms can analyze patterns in solar and wind data over time, optimizing energy forecasts and operational strategies. For instance, machine learning models can train on historical data to predict solar irradiance under various atmospheric conditions, enabling better planning for energy usage.

Communication with Earth regarding energy management can also be streamlined using Linux systems, providing real-time feedback on energy production, consumption, and battery levels. Relay satellites equipped with Linux-based systems can facilitate this exchange of information, ensuring that energy strategies evolve based on mission control recommendations.

In conclusion, effectively addressing energy resources and management for Martian expeditions hinges on harnessing renewable energy options tailored to the planet's unique conditions. The combination of solar power, potential wind energy, ISRU technologies, and robust energy management systems embodies a forward-thinking approach to sustainable exploration. By leveraging Linux's adaptability and resourcefulness, researchers and engineers can establish frameworks that optimize energy usage, ensure reliability, and support the long-term objectives of human and robotic missions on Mars, ultimately laying the groundwork for a sustainable presence on the Red Planet.

4.5. Artificial Intelligence and Automation

The intersection of artificial intelligence (AI) and automation is revolutionizing the way we approach space exploration, serving as a crucial enabling technology for missions to Mars and beyond. As we prepare to send robots, rovers, and eventually humans to the Red Planet, it becomes imperative to understand how AI and automation can enhance operational capabilities, dataset processing, and real-time decision-making, especially in environments characterized by uncertainty and extreme conditions.

At the forefront of this technological evolution, AI offers the promise of intelligent systems capable of performing complex tasks autonomously. In the context of Martian exploration, where communication with Earth can experience significant delays—ranging from a few minutes to over twenty minutes depending on the relative positions of the planets—autonomy is essential. Mars rovers, such as Curiosity and Perseverance, have already begun to showcase the benefits of autonomous navigational capabilities. Running on sophisticated Linux-based operating systems, these rovers utilize AI algorithms to process sensor data, assess their surroundings, and make navigation decisions without waiting for instructions from mission control. As we move forward, the integration of more advanced AI systems into the Linux architecture will enhance these capabilities, allowing for more advanced interpretation of environmental data and more intricate autonomous behavior.

One of the key areas where AI is making strides is in environmental modeling and hazard detection. The Martian landscape presents numerous challenges, including rough terrain, sudden obstacles, and changing weather conditions. By utilizing machine learning techniques, systems can be trained to recognize topographical features and evaluate risk factors, enabling rovers to traverse these complex environments safely and efficiently. These deep learning models can analyze vast amounts of data collected from various sensors, refining their predictive capabilities and improving the accuracy of autonomous decisions made en route to their objectives.

Automation, in tandem with AI, plays a crucial role in managing the vast quantities of data collected during Martian missions. Rovers and landers generate a plethora of information—ranging from geological samples to atmospheric readings—where human data management is impractical. Automated systems can process, classify, and store this information in real time. For instance, designing Linux-based software that incorporates automation for data transmission can streamline workflows, ensuring that critical observations are prioritized for immediate transmission back to Earth. By implementing automated data retrieval and processing systems, scientists can access results in near real-time, allowing them to adapt experiments and missions dynamically based on incoming data.

Furthermore, AI-driven predictive analytics add another layer of functionality essential for survival on Mars. Missions must contend with uncertainties, including the likelihood of dust storms, temperature fluctuations, and radiation exposure. AI systems can utilize historical data to forecast these events and optimize mission strategies accordingly. For example, by predicting when a dust storm is likely to occur, rovers can autonomously navigate to optimal locations to wait it out, or adjust their power management systems to conserve energy in anticipation of diminished solar power collection.

In the robotics domain, the convergence of AI and automation fortifies the resilience of systems deployed on Mars. Robots designed for repairs, maintenance, or scientific experiments will benefit from enhanced decision-making capabilities, allowing them to execute complex operations autonomously while minimizing the need for human intervention. For instance, robotic arms controlled by advanced AI can perform delicate tasks such as material samples collection or manipulation of experimental apparatus without direct oversight. Such autonomy is crucial for missions where human presence is limited, ensuring that scientific objectives can be accomplished consistently over extended periods.

The potential for AI and automation in Martian missions extends into collaborative frameworks between multiple operators. As teams of rovers and drones work in concert, each unit can operate semi-autonomously while communicating with one another to achieve mission objectives more effectively. AI algorithms can facilitate inter-robot collaboration, enabling systems to divide tasks based on strengths or current operational limitations, optimizing research outputs, and improving task efficiency.

As we design and implement these systems, understanding the ethics of employing AI technologies in space exploration must also be prioritized. Ensuring that AI systems behave predictably and adhere to established protocols is essential. Strategies must be developed to limit error rates and enhance system accountability—especially for autonomous decision-making in environments vastly different from Earth.

Cybersecurity measures are another critical consideration. The autonomous nature of these systems means that robust security protocols must be in place to safeguard them against potential vulnerabilities while operating in interconnected configurations. Security solutions would need to be integrated into Linux systems to protect against cyber threats that might exploit the autonomy of robotic systems. The open-source nature of Linux provides a unique opportunity for rapid community-driven enhancements to security frameworks, ensuring that AI and automation can be implemented without compromising the mission's integrity.

In summary, crossing the technological threshold with AI and automation embodies a pivotal shift in how Martian exploration will be conducted. By harnessing these technologies, we can create intelligent systems that operate autonomously, adapt to unforeseen circumstances, and manage vast amounts of data. As we prepare for human and robotic missions to Mars, the integration of AI and automation into Linux will not just enhance our capabilities; it will redefine the approach to exploration itself, opening up new opportunities for scientific research and fundamentally altering the landscape of interplanetary missions.

5. Preparing Linux for Martian Experiences

5.1. Adapting to Environmental Extremes

In the quest for human exploration of Mars, one of the most significant challenges revolves around the need for technology to adapt to the planet's extreme environmental conditions. The Martian atmosphere, characterized by low pressure, high levels of radiation, and severe temperature fluctuations, presents unique demands on operational systems, including Linux-based setups. To ensure that Linux can effectively serve its purpose in these challenging circumstances, a multifaceted approach focusing on adaptation and resilience is paramount.

First and foremost, it is essential to understand the Martian environment. With an atmosphere that is 95% carbon dioxide and only about 1% the density of Earth's atmosphere, any systems deployed on Mars must be designed to operate within a vacuum-like environment where the risk of decompression is significant. This requires tightly sealed hardware that can withstand external pressure changes and prevent the intrusion of dust and sand, which are prevalent due to frequent dust storms. Linux systems need to be optimized for monitoring these environmental conditions continuously, ensuring that they operate effectively even when faced with the harshest atmospheres.

Another critical factor to consider is the extreme temperature variation on Mars, where daytime temperatures can soar to 20 degrees Celsius (68 degrees Fahrenheit), while nighttime temperatures can plummet to –73 degrees Celsius (-100 degrees Fahrenheit). Such variations demand robust thermal management solutions. Linux must be equipped with monitoring and control systems that can regulate temperature within hardware components, ensuring that they remain functional and do not overheat during the day nor freeze at night. Efficient coding practices within Linux can facilitate the management of power consumption, reducing heat generation during non-peak operational periods and preserving battery life.

Moreover, addressing the risk of radiation exposure is vital for any technology intended for Martian missions. The lack of a protective magnetic field on Mars results in higher radiation levels compared to Earth. This poses risks to both human health and to the electronics housed within mission equipment. Linux systems should incorporate radiation-hardened components to protect against these effects. This hardening process may include physical shielding measures, software protective features that monitor equipment health, and the implementation of redundancy to allow systems to continue functioning even if some components are compromised.

Dust storms present another significant environmental extreme on Mars and can obscure sunlight for weeks at a time, affecting solar-powered systems and potentially impacting the reliability of energy systems. The Linux-based architecture must be capable of integrating real-time data feeds concerning weather conditions, enabling proactive maneuvers, such as repositioning solar panels, activating alternative power sources, or performing cleaning routines to maintain operational capabilities. This real-time adaptability is essential for maintaining continuous power supply, particularly for critical operations like life support or scientific data collection.

The navigation challenges presented by the Martian terrain—often rocky, uneven, and full of sudden drops—require advanced processing capabilities to ensure safe mobility. Linux can be augmented with AI and machine learning algorithms to enhance predictive capabilities, guiding rovers and other unmanned systems in real time as they traverse unpredictable landscapes. The algorithms could facilitate hazard detection and route optimization, allowing for autonomous decisions on navigation without relying on intermittent communication with Earth.

In addition, Linux systems must be designed for reliable operation over long periods with minimal maintenance, addressing the limited accessibility for repair and the need for the longevity of components under extreme conditions. This is where fault tolerance comes into play. Linux can be customized to include built-in diagnostic tools that intervene as soon as anomalies are detected—whether through software recalibrations or hardware replacements where feasible —ensuring that the operating system continues to function, thus maintaining the mission's objectives.

Another key element is the need for a modular Linux configuration that allows for the selective use of different software components based on the tasks at hand. For example, specific modules may be built for data analysis, communication management, or even environmental monitoring, providing a tailored approach that optimizes resource use and minimizes power consumption. These customizable modules can be deployed dynamically in response to changing mission parameters or environmental conditions, ensuring that Linux remains agile and effective under varying circumstances.

Finally, it is crucial to establish comprehensive testing protocols that simulate Martian environmental extremes before deploying technology onto the planet. By conducting thorough simulations of temperature differentials, radiation exposure, and dust environment impact scenarios on Earth, developers can iterate and enhance the Linux configurations to ensure maximum resilience and robustness under actual Martian conditions.

In summary, adapting Linux to meet the environmental extremes of Mars is a complex undertaking that requires a multifaceted approach focusing on thermal management, shielding against radiation, automation capabilities for navigating harsh terrains, and the preservation of system integrity through redundancy and modularity. By employing these strategies, we can prepare Linux to serve as a reliable operating system capable of supporting human exploration and establishing a sustainable presence on Mars, ultimately paving the way for humanity's future in space.

5.2. Real-Time System Requirements

The concept of real-time system requirements is integral to the success of any space mission, especially those destined for Mars, where environmental unpredictability and communication delays necessitate swift and effective responses from onboard systems. The unique challenges posed by Martian conditions, alongside the inherent limitations of interplanetary communication, underscore the importance of developing a robust architecture that can accommodate real-time processing needs. Drawing from the capabilities of Linux as a flexible and adaptive operating system, various strategies and implementations can be configured to enhance the performance and reliability of systems tasked with handling real-time requirements on the Red Planet.

To begin with, it's crucial to delineate what constitutes a real-time system in the context of Martian exploration. Real-time systems are characterized by their ability to process data and respond to inputs within a predetermined time interval, effectively coordinating actions based on sensor data or situational changes. For instance, a rover navigating Martian terrain must instantly interpret the data received from its cameras and sensors to avoid obstacles or adapt its behavior to shifting conditions. This responsive nature is paramount where delayed reactions could lead to catastrophic failures or missed scientific opportunities.

Linux, as a versatile operating system, offers real-time extensions that can be utilized to enhance its capability to function in real-time operational contexts. These extensions enable developers to create applications that prioritize urgent tasks through advanced scheduling algorithms, allowing the system to allocate CPU resources efficiently. By employing priority-based scheduling, critical processes—such as those responsible for navigation and environmental monitoring—can be guaranteed necessary computing resources to execute tasks with minimal latency, ensuring that responses to immediate threats or circumstances are swift and accurate.

Consistency in task performance is another significant aspect concerning real-time systems. With the unpredictable nature of the Martian landscape, it is crucial that software applications maintain a high level of performance reliability under varying conditions. Linux supports mechanisms for determining task execution times, tracking maximum latency, and providing insights into system performance that help developers identify potential bottlenecks. By optimizing software through testing frameworks that simulate Martian environmental pressures, engineers can ensure that mission-critical applications perform consistently over time, even amid the unpredictable stresses of the Martian atmosphere.

Furthermore, implementing a modular architecture within Linux serves to enhance its real-time capabilities. By breaking down software into multiple components or modules, mission systems can be adjusted in response to specific real-time requirements that emerge during exploration. This modularity allows for the independent updating and maintenance of subsystems without impacting the overall operational integrity, thus facilitating resilient and adaptive system design. For instance, if an enhanced navigation algorithm needs to be deployed quickly during Martian operations, it can be introduced as a new module while preserving the legacy systems' functions until they can be safely updated.

Considerable importance must also be directed towards data throughput and management. As Mars missions involve a plethora of sensors, cameras, and actuators generating vast amounts of data, the Linux operating system must be configured to handle not only real-time processing demands but also manage data effectively. Employing data prioritization strategies can ensure that the most critical information is processed and analyzed first, enhancing decision-making. Systems established with Linux could leverage advanced buffering techniques that temporarily hold sensor data while the system processes higher-priority data streams, thereby optimizing throughput without compromising the integrity of timely information.

The unique challenges posed by long communication delays between Earth and Mars mean that relying on mission control for real-time assistance is not feasible. This scenario necessitates a higher degree of autonomy in onboard systems, placing the development of sophisticated AI algorithms front and center. By incorporating AI-driven decision-making frameworks within the Linux architecture, rovers and other autonomous agents can react to swiftly changing scenarios based on pre-established criteria and learned behaviors. For example, a rover equipped with a learning algorithm that adapts over time can autonomously better recognize hazardous terrain, improving both navigation safety and mission success.

An equally critical consideration involves real-time health monitoring systems capable of assessing the operational status of onboard components. Linux can be configured to support diagnostic applications that routinely check the health of mission systems, whether evaluating power availability, tracking system temperatures, or monitoring the functionality of critical sensors. This proactive approach to system health management contributes to the resilience of operations as systems can address faults or anomalies before they escalate into mission-threatening scenarios.

Lastly, real-time system requirements demand comprehensive testing protocols to ensure that systems are robust enough to operate under actual conditions on Mars. Engineers can simulate various Martian scenarios to evaluate the performance of real-time systems, identifying potential failure points and optimizing response strategies. These extensive test simulations serve as a crucial step, supplying data that guides engineers in refining algorithms and improving overall system performance to meet the specific needs posed by the Martian environment.

In summary, the real-time system requirements vital for Martian missions hinge on developing flexible, reliable, and efficient technological solutions capable of rapid response to dynamic environmental conditions. Utilizing Linux's rich capabilities—enhanced through real-time extensions, modular architecture, strategic data management, AI integration, health monitoring, and rigorous testing—ensures that mission systems can operate effectively and autonomously, securing the success of exploratory endeavors on Mars. By addressing these real-time needs, we construct a resilient framework for future exploration, enabling humanity to push the boundaries of space beyond our planetary home.

5.3. Virtualization in Space Contexts

In the context of space exploration, virtualization offers unique benefits and presents formidable challenges, establishing itself as a pivotal technology for managing resources effectively on extraterrestrial missions. By allowing multiple operating systems to run concurrently on a single hardware platform, virtualization creates an efficient environment that is adaptable to the ever-changing needs of missions to Mars and beyond.

The primary advantage of virtualization lies in its resource efficiency. Space missions often operate under stringent hardware constraints, utilizing a limited number of devices that must be capable of a variety of functions. Virtualization allows for the consolidation of hardware resources, meaning that a single physical machine can host multiple virtual machines, each running its own operating system tailored to specific tasks. This not only optimizes resource usage but also simplifies hardware requirements, which is crucial when considering the weight and volume limitations of spacecraft destined for Mars.

For instance, a single rover equipped with virtualization capabilities could potentially manage different operating environments for various applications—one instance of Linux for navigational tasks, another for scientific data collection, and yet another for communications. Each of these virtual machines can operate independently while sharing the underlying hardware, effectively allowing for greater functionality without the overhead of deploying multiple separate physical systems. In the harsh Martian landscape, this means that a single Rover could perform a wide array of complex tasks while reducing the risk of failure correlated with a more extensive hardware setup.

Moreover, virtualization facilitates system isolation. In a mission-critical environment, ensuring that tasks remain compartmentalized is essential to maintain overall system integrity. Should a virtual machine encounter a failure due to an anomaly, it can be isolated from the others, ensuring that the remaining operations are unaffected. This isolation can be particularly advantageous for mission control, which needs reliable systems that can recover gracefully from errors without causing a cascade of failures across other applications.

However, deploying virtualization technologies in space also presents significant challenges. The Martian environment poses unique threats, including radiation, extreme temperature fluctuations, and dust accumulation. These factors can affect both the hardware and the virtualization layer itself. Spacecraft electronics need to be radiation-hardened to withstand cosmic rays that can cause data corruption and hardware malfunctions—issues that may jeopardize the stability of virtualized environments reliant on that hardware. Furthermore, the virtualization software must be robust enough to handle potential interference and ensure that virtual machines can operate seamlessly, even in the presence of hardware anomalies.

Latency in communications between virtualized systems also poses challenges. In real-time applications, especially those pertinent to rovers navigating unpredictable terrains, the need for immediate responsiveness is paramount. The processing overhead introduced by virtualization can create delays in data processing that are unacceptable in scenarios requiring instant decision-making capabilities. To mitigate this risk, careful optimization of virtual machine configurations, including the allocation of processing resources, is essential to balance efficiency and performance.

Additionally, implementing interconnectivity among various virtual machines within a single hardware platform introduces complexity related to networking and data management. Ensuring effective communication between virtual machines and maintaining synchronization is critical, especially when multiple systems operate autonomously in real-time applications. Linux-based systems can facilitate robust networking features through built-in support for virtual networking, enabling virtual machines to share data effectively while adhering to stringent security protocols.

Another aspect to consider is the management of software upgrades and maintenance in a virtualized environment. The notion of rapidly iterating on software in response to findings or emerging needs is paramount, yet the layered architecture created by virtualization can introduce complexities. Linux allows for various containerization technologies (like Docker) that can be exceptionally beneficial for managing software versions, enabling streamlined, isolated deployments and rollbacks without affecting the overall virtualized architecture.

As we prepare for Martian missions, it becomes increasingly clear that adopting virtualization brings both opportunities and challenges. To maximize the benefits, strategic planning, testing, and robust implementation of virtualization technologies must be approached with a clear understanding of the unique requirements posed by the extraterrestrial environment. By leveraging Linux's flexibility and adaptability in creating virtualized platforms tailored to Mars, we can enhance mission capabilities while ensuring robustness and resilience in the face of the unknown. The strategic use of virtualization may very well redefine the operational efficacy of systems deployed beyond our terrestrial realm, allowing humanity to explore the cosmos in ambitious, innovative ways. The successful mitigation of challenges associated with virtualization could pave the way for even more sophisticated systems, laying the groundwork for future explorations not only on Mars but throughout the solar system and beyond.

5.4. Mitigating Cosmic Radiation Effects

To effectively mitigate the effects of cosmic radiation for missions involving Linux-powered technology on Mars, a thorough understanding of the nature of cosmic radiation is essential. Cosmic radiation stems primarily from high-energy particles emitted by the sun, as well as from galactic sources beyond our solar system. These particles can penetrate various materials and interact with electronic components, leading to malfunctions or catastrophic failures. The impact of this radiation is especially significant for spacecraft and rovers where the electronic systems are critical to mission success.

One primary mitigation strategy involves employing radiation-hardened materials in the construction of hardware. Radiation-hardened components are specifically designed to endure higher radiation levels without degradation. This can include using specialized semiconductors, shielding devices with lead or other heavy materials, and employing redundant systems to minimize the impact of any single point of failure caused by radiation exposure. Additionally, integrating radiation-tolerant software protocols into Linux can help manage the resilience and responsiveness of systems affected by radiation-induced anomalies.

Another crucial strategy focuses on the design of effective shielding around sensitive electronic components. This shielding can be implemented through layered constructions that utilize a combination of materials to provide protection against different types of radiation. For example, polyethylene is effective against protons and neutrons, while heavier metals like lead block high-energy photons. An intelligent Linux-based monitoring system can continuously assess radiation levels within spacecraft and adaptively manage the operation of sensitive systems based on real-time data, which would allow the software to enter a safe mode during extreme conditions.

The ability to monitor and assess environmental radiation levels is another pivotal strategy. Utilizing Linux's capabilities for integrating sensor systems enables the continuous collection of data regarding cosmic radiation exposure. By deploying radiation sensors within the spacecraft's design, engineers can program Linux to trigger alerts if radiation levels exceed safe thresholds, allowing operators to take preventative measures or adjust mission parameters accordingly. This sort of proactive monitoring can enhance the robustness of any missions deployed to Mars.

Implementing redundancy in both hardware and software is vital in the context of cosmic radiation. Creating backup systems to take over in the event of primary system failure due to radiation damage is an effective resilience method. This could involve duplicating critical sensors or employing different algorithms for data processing within

Linux, allowing the mission to continue if one path is compromised. In practice, this might mean having multiple Linux instances ready to assume control should the primary instance exhibit signs of radiation-induced corruption.

Automation and autonomous decision-making algorithms embedded within Linux can improve the speed and reliability of response mechanisms to detected radiation threats. By utilizing artificial intelligence, systems can determine the optimal course of action for mission success. These algorithms could be developed to modify operational procedures based solely on the level of incoming radiation, such as altering operational timings to maximize efficiency during periods of higher radiation exposure, effectively managing energy consumption while protecting vital components.

Moreover, simulating cosmic radiation effects on Linux systems during the development and testing phases is crucial. Utilizing facilities that can replicate the types of radiation exposure expected on Mars allows developers to rigorously test their systems prior to actual deployment. By conducting experiments on hardware initialized with customized Linux distributions, engineers can observe how systems behave under heightened radiation and make adjustments accordingly to ensure robustness when the systems are deployed in the field.

Furthermore, machine learning techniques can be utilized within the Linux environment to analyze historical radiation data, potentially predicting periods of increased cosmic activity based on past measurements. By identifying trends and correlations within this data, engineers can design systems capable of adaptive responses that enhance survivability in radiation-heavy periods, such as implementing strategic shutdowns or power conservation techniques anticipating changes in cosmic radiation levels.

Finally, exploring partnerships with space agencies and research institutions can facilitate enhanced knowledge-sharing regarding cosmic radiation mitigation techniques. By leveraging existing research and development efforts on hardware, software, and innovative shielding techniques, Linux can be optimized collectively, resulting in advanced operational systems that not only withstand radiation effects but also maximize their efficiency through collaboration and shared findings.

In conclusion, mitigating cosmic radiation effects within Linux-operated systems for Mars missions requires a comprehensive strategy blending hardware enhancements, real-time monitoring, redundancy, intelligent software design, testing, and international collaboration. By prioritizing these strategies, we can ensure the resilience and reliability of systems that are crucial for the successful exploration and eventual habitation of Martian territory, even in the face of extreme cosmic challenges.

5.5. Robustness and Resilience Under Stress

Robustness and resilience are critical characteristics that Linux-based systems must embody when deployed in the extreme conditions of Mars. The harsh Martian environment, coupled with the demands of extended missions, presents unique challenges that could easily jeopardize the success of any operation. To ensure reliability and effectiveness, engineers and developers must implement a framework that incorporates a range of strategies aimed at enhancing system robustness and resilience under stress.

One of the primary considerations for building robust systems revolves around the harsh environmental conditions on Mars. The extreme temperature fluctuations—ranging from scorching heat during the day to bone-chilling cold at night—require that Linux systems are equipped with advanced thermal management protocols. Custom algorithms will need to monitor operating temperatures in real-time, allowing the systems to adapt operational states to optimize performance while preserving hardware longevity. The use of thermal insulation materials alongside intelligent software solutions can further shield sensitive components from temperature extremes.

Another essential aspect of resilience is the capacity to withstand radiation exposure. As Mars lacks a protective magnetic field and its atmosphere offers minimal shielding, cosmic and solar radiation could lead to significant electronic disruptions. To enhance robustness, systems should incorporate radiation-hardened components designed specifically for space environments. Moreover, implementing error-checking protocols within the Linux environment can help manage and correct errors that arise from radiation effects, ensuring that critical operations are safeguarded against potential disruptions.

Moreover, redundancy is a fundamental strategy to bolster both robustness and resilience. This includes the dual deployment of critical components, whether they are payload sensors, navigational units, or data storage solutions. In the event a primary unit fails or experiences degradation due to Martian conditions, a backup can seamlessly take over without operational interruptions. Linux's flexibility allows developers to create a structure where multiple instances of essential services can run concurrently, ensuring continual availability and functionality.

Data integrity in space missions is another area requiring reinforced resiliency. High volumes of data will be generated throughout missions on Mars, necessitating a comprehensive data management strategy within Linux. Implementing robust error detection, correction protocols, and data redundancy systems will ensure that critical information remains intact despite potential hardware failures or environmental factors. File systems designed for high resilience, capable of maintaining data integrity even under distressing conditions, are crucial for supporting mission objectives.

Continuous monitoring and predictive maintenance must complement the above strategies. Linux systems can integrate advanced sensor networks that evaluate the health of hardware components in real-time. By establishing thresholds for various performance metrics and leveraging machine learning algorithms, systems can predict when components may fail and perform automated maintenance actions, thus preempting issues before they escalate. This proactive approach minimizes downtime and reinforces mission continuity, a crucial factor for success in the isolation of Martian expeditions.

Networking and communication resilience must also be considered. Given the significant latencies and potential communication interruptions with Earth, Linux systems need to manage data locally before prioritizing information for transmission. Systems that can operate autonomously yet still maintain the capability of sharing critical information during solar conjunctions or power loss scenarios will ensure that operations remain on track despite communication challenges.

Security is often an overlooked aspect of robustness, especially concerning the integrity of commands and control systems on Mars. By integrating security protocols unique to Linux, systems will be able to validate and authenticate all incoming and outgoing communications with mission control. This cybersecurity layer is critical to preventing potential threats—whether from natural cosmic events or unauthorized interference—that could compromise mission systems.

The adaptability of Linux itself is vital to its robustness in the Martian context. By utilizing containerization technologies or virtual environments, developers can establish modular applications that can be easily updated, swapped out, or replaced to respond to evolving mission needs. This enables a computing environment that can adjust dynamically as new technologies become available or as operational requirements shift due to changing conditions on the surface of Mars.

Extensive testing on Earth of software and hardware in simulated Martian environments must also be a cornerstone of the planning phase. By rigorously stress-testing systems under replicated Martian conditions—such as extreme temperatures, pressure differentials, and radiation exposure—engineers can gain critical insights into performance limits and potential system vulnerabilities. This phase will help refine and enhance the robustness of deployed systems before they embark on their journey to Mars.

In summary, the emphasis on robustness and resilience under stress for Linux systems destined for Mars involves a multifaceted approach that encompasses environmental adaptation, advanced thermal and radiation management, redundancy, data integrity, autonomous maintenance, secure communications, and adaptive technologies. Each of these strategies plays a crucial role in safeguarding mission success, fostering an operating environment that not only survives but thrives amid the challenges posed by the formidable Martian landscape. As humanity embarks on this ambitious quest for exploration, the resilience of Linux-based systems will be essential in paving the way for technological advancement and discovery on our nearest planetary neighbor.

6. Implementing Linux on Mars Missions

6.1. Initial Testing and Simulations

In preparing for missions to Mars, the initial phases of testing and simulation are paramount to ensure that Linux and its associated systems can operate reliably in such hostile conditions. The process involves rigorous checks and assessments designed to mimic the Martian environment as closely as possible here on Earth. This approach allows developers and engineers to identify potential weaknesses in hardware and software before deployment, thus enhancing the overall resilience and functionality of mission systems.

The first step in the initial testing phase is to establish a baseline understanding of how the chosen Linux distribution will perform under simulated Martian conditions. This involves reproducing the extreme temperatures, low atmospheric pressure, radiation exposure, and dust accumulation typical of Mars. Specialized facilities capable of creating vacuum-like environments are used, allowing for configuration tests of both hardware and software.

Temperature regulation is one crucial area of focus during initial tests. Linux-based systems must be equipped to handle significant fluctuations that can range from plus 20 degrees Celsius in daylight to minus 73 degrees Celsius at night. Environmental chambers simulate these conditions by subjecting the hardware to a variety of thermal cycles while running Linux applications designed to monitor hardware performance and response times. Engineers closely observe metrics such as component temperatures, system stability, and overall performance to assess whether the hardware can withstand prolonged exposure without failure.

Testing for low pressure is equally critical. The Martian atmosphere, with its minuscule pressure of less than 1% that of Earth, poses serious challenges for moisture and the integrity of sealed systems. Tests are conducted to ensure that all components can operate and communicate effectively in a vacuum environment. This includes maintaining functionality in sensor readings, data processing tasks, and communication protocols, ensuring the integrity of data pathways remains intact despite the reduced atmospheric pressure.

Simulations also explore how hardware responds under significant radiation exposure. Spacecraft and rover electronics must be robust enough to resist the high-energy particles prevalent on Mars. Using radiation sources, Linux systems are tested to measure performance while subjected to radiation levels akin to those experienced beyond Earth's protective atmosphere. During these simulations, stress tests identify how errors manifest in the system's operation, allowing developers to refine mitigation strategies, such as employing error-correcting software routines and redundant hardware setups.

In addition to environmental simulations, data generation procedures are tested extensively. As mission time may require extensive data collection and transmission, the Linux operating system must be capable of effectively managing large datasets. While simulating Mars conditions, environments are created that mimic the limitations of bandwidth and latency faced during interplanetary communication. Using satellite relay models, Linux applications simulate the sending and receiving of data to build resilience during potential communication disruptions. The focus is on ensuring that all systems can process and cache data efficiently even when connectivity is intermittent, a necessity given that communications can experience delays of up to 24 minutes or more.

Simulation tests also incorporate scenarios involving exploration missions, including navigation challenges and obstacle detection. Robotics and AI systems programmed on Linux are put through their paces in controlled environments replicating the Martian landscape. Using various scenarios, such as rocky terrains or sudden obstacles, engineers assess the real-time computer vision capability of rovers and the algorithms governing their movement. These tests are crucial for evaluating both autonomy and the effectiveness of the AI algorithms in decision-making under pressure.

To complement these simulations, concurrent real-world testing on prototypes is also conducted. Building physical models of rovers or landers that are close representatives of future Mars vehicles allows for hands-on testing in environments that cannot entirely replicate Martian conditions. These prototypes undergo functional tests such as navigational trials, sensor integration, and power distribution management under various conditions, closely monitored and recorded using the customized Linux systems controlling them.

After completing the initial round of testing and simulations, results from these exercises must be thoroughly analyzed to refine designs and improve system performance. Feedback gathered from the testing phases serves as a basis for iterative development cycles, enabling engineers to enhance operating procedures and algorithms before the systems are ultimately deployed.

As we continue to move towards ambitious missions on Mars, the emphasis on initial testing and simulations under carefully controlled conditions offers invaluable insights. Through this process, developers can optimize Linux for robustness and adaptability, ensuring that our technological foothold on Mars can withstand the myriad challenges posed by the unforgiving Martian environment. Each phase of this preparation reinforces the commitment to mission success, innovation, and safe exploration of our neighboring planet, setting a firm foundation for the future of humanity in space.

6.2. Deployment Strategies and Protocols

The deployment strategies and protocols for Linux systems on Martian missions necessitate a carefully designed approach that encompasses thorough planning, execution, and ongoing adjustments. As we aim for successful exploration and potential colonization of Mars, establishing effective deployment strategies—rooted in practical methodologies and resilient frameworks—will ensure that technology performs optimally in the unique and challenging Martian environment.

First and foremost, a foundational step in deployment involves rigorous assessment of the mission objectives and operational requirements. Defining clear goals—whether for scientific research, resource monitoring, habitat establishment, or technological validation—will guide the selection of appropriate Linux configurations, hardware platforms, and application deployments. This initial understanding lays the groundwork for developing specific deployment protocols tailored to the anticipated conditions on Mars.

Once objectives are established, a phased approach to deployment can be enacted. It is beneficial to begin with a limited scope, deploying smaller components or systems in stages, a method akin to an incremental rollout. This allows for controlled testing and validation on Martian surfaces, providing insights that inform subsequent steps. For instance, launching a prototype rover with a Linux-based operating system can serve as a pilot mission, enabling engineers to assess performance under real Martian conditions. Over time, additional systems—such as habitat monitoring or environmental sensors—can be deployed based on insights gained from the initial rounds.

Furthermore, developing the specific logistics for transportation of Linux-powered systems can significantly impact execution. Assemblies must be designed to withstand the harsh conditions of space travel, including significant vibration and temperature variance. Strategies should include securing sensitive components and using protective casings that can endure launch stresses. Pre-launch simulations will be critical to validating that entire setups performed correctly during transport and that each component will function as intended.

In conjunction with transportation logistics, effective communication protocols for operational deployment must also be solidified early on. Given the inherent delays in communications between Mars and Earth—ranging from four to twenty-four minutes—autonomy becomes paramount. Thus, systems deployed on Mars must be self-sufficient, capable of making decisions based on pre-programmed algorithms within the Linux framework. The deployment protocols should specify how data is collected, processed, and potentially relayed back to Earth for analysis, ensuring that autonomous decision-making processes are embedded into system operations.

Once Linux systems are deployed on Mars, the next stage involves ongoing monitoring and dynamic adjustment of those systems. Continuous system health checks and performance diagnostics must be integrated into the deployment strategy, facilitated by Linux's inherent capabilities for logging and data collection. Engineers should implement feedback mechanisms that allow systems to report their operational status periodically, making them capable of detecting anomalies or performance issues autonomously. Utilizing machine learning algorithms and predictive analytics, these systems can identify potential failures before they escalate, providing critical insights for maintenance or recalibration.

Incorporating a robust set of adaptive protocols further enhances deployment strategies. This should focus on enabling decentralized decision-making wherein individual components can act and adapt based on localized data. For example, if a rover identifies an obstacle or a geological feature of interest, it should autonomously adjust its sampling methodology or modify its route without awaiting commands from mission control. Flexibility in these protocols allows for swift adaptations to unforeseen challenges typically encountered in the unpredictable Martian terrain.

Comprehensive training and documentation must be included as part of the deployment protocols. Given that various teams and personnel may interact with the deployed systems remotely, well-structured training resources ensure proper usage and troubleshooting of Linux-based technologies. This forms a cohesive understanding of operations, troubleshooting procedures, and contingency measures among diverse teams involved in ongoing missions, creating a unified approach to mission execution.

Collaboration between mission-planning teams and operational personnel is essential as well. This synergy assists in harmonizing communication between developers and field operators and ensures that feedback from the operational phase swiftly informs any necessary adjustments to system software or hardware. Such alignment fosters an agile development environment where iterative refinements can be made without lengthy delays.

Lastly, staying prepared for the eventualities of Martian conditions —such as dust storms or extreme temperatures—should influence deployment strategies and protocols. Incorporating redundancy and failover systems within the Linux framework ensures continuous operations, thereby enhancing resilience. This redundancy can span from having backup power systems to employing redundant sensors that maintain data collection streams even in the face of localized failures.

In summary, implementing deployment strategies and protocols for Linux systems on Mars requires a meticulous, multi-layered approach. By engaging in thorough assessments of operational requirements, adopting a phased deployment strategy, ensuring robust communication protocols, and fostering ongoing adaptability, we can create a reliable technological foundation that thrives amidst the challenges of the Martian environment. As exploration endeavors unfold, these protocols will provide the necessary roadmap to support successful missions and pave the way for humanity's extended presence on the Red Planet.

6.3. Feedback Loops and Iterations

In the realm of software development, feedback loops and iterative processes play a pivotal role in refining technology, especially when preparing systems for the demanding conditions of Mars. The dynamic nature of space exploration necessitates continuous evaluation and enhancement of the operating systems and software powering rovers, habitats, and scientific instruments. The iterative development model allows teams to adapt quickly to new findings, environmental challenges, and mission requirements, ensuring that Linux systems are optimally configured for the rigors of interplanetary operation.

The foundation of effective feedback mechanisms begins with establishing clear objectives for each mission phase. Whether the goal is data collection, autonomous navigation, or environmental monitoring, defining specific success criteria provides a roadmap for system performance evaluation. Operational data must be meticulously recorded, capturing metrics such as processing times, error rates, energy consumption, and system responsiveness. This data serves as a critical input for subsequent iterations, allowing mission planners to identify areas of improvement and prioritize enhancements that directly impact mission success.

Simulations and real-world testing provide an invaluable context for gathering feedback. As systems are subjected to Martian-like conditions, engineers can observe how Linux-based applications perform under stress. The challenges posed by thermal extremes, radiation exposure, and dust accumulation yield insights into hardware durability and software functionality. For instance, if a rover experiences unexpected latency while processing sensor data, engineers can analyze logs and system outputs to identify bottlenecks in the Linux kernel or application layer. Armed with this information, the development team can implement optimizations such as refining algorithms, enhancing task prioritization, or modifying parameters that govern resource allocation.

Moreover, the role of automated monitoring systems within Linux environments cannot be overstated. By integrating real-time monitoring tools, teams can create feedback loops that continuously evaluate system health and performance. These tools can deploy alerts and diagnostics based on predefined thresholds, informing developers of emerging issues before they escalate into significant problems. Should a rover onboard system detect an anomaly, feedback can trigger automated checks or adjustments, enhancing resilience in the face of potential failures. This proactive approach bolsters mission continuity and ensures that systems can adapt to challenges as they arise.

Collaboration across interdisciplinary teams is essential in leveraging feedback effectively. As mission objectives evolve, engineers, scientists, and software developers must communicate and share insights transparently. Regular debriefs and progress assessments create opportunities for cross-pollination of ideas, fostering a culture of iterative improvement. In practice, this might involve integrating suggestions from scientists who utilize the data being collected into software adjustments that enhance data retrieval or presentation formats, ensuring greater accessibility and utility in scientific contexts.

The world of open-source software development, which is the backbone of Linux, further enriches these feedback dynamics. A collaborative community of developers and experts from diverse backgrounds can contribute their knowledge and insights, accelerating the iteration process. When issues are identified in one application or subsystem, the wider community can issue patches or develop solutions that benefit not just the original mission but potentially future missions. This aspect of rapid iteration transcends individual efforts and promotes a collective advancement that is invaluable in the field of space exploration.

The practice of conducting after-action reviews and post-mission analyses is another vital component of an effective iterative process. Once a mission concludes, an exhaustive evaluation of system performance, operational successes, and shortcomings can yield lessons that inform future developments. By documenting findings and revisiting the original mission objectives in light of collected data, engineers can ensure that future iterations build on the strengths of past missions while addressing their weaknesses.

Additionally, simulation environments often need to undergo iterative improvements themselves, adjusting operating parameters and scenarios based on real mission outcomes. By implementing insights gained from actual operations, developers can enhance the fidelity of simulation tools to better prepare for future challenges. This approach not only refines the testing phase but also contributes more accurately to the predictive modeling of system behaviors in Martian contexts.

Finally, adopting a mindset of continuous improvement helps create an environment where iteration is ingrained in the culture of development teams. By embracing the philosophy that every component, function, and process can be enhanced, mission planners foster an atmosphere that prioritizes innovation, value-added modifications, and resilience against the unpredictability of space environments. As we prepare for the profound tasks ahead on Mars, instilling this iterative spirit within the Linux-based systems underpinning exploration becomes critical—the ultimate goal is not merely surviving on another planet but ensuring that humanity thrives in its quest to explore the cosmos.

As we look ahead, a firm understanding of how feedback loops facilitate iterative improvement will prove invaluable. The lessons learned from each phase of exploration will directly inform the designs and protocols of subsequent missions, ensuring that Linux evolves in tandem with the needs of the community, the science being conducted, and the environments being conquered—ultimately reaffirming its role as a cornerstone of our efforts to extend human presence beyond Earth.

6.4. Integrated Systems Overview

In the overarching strategy for Mars missions, the integration of Linux within the broader mission framework is a critical aspect that ensures various systems operate cohesively and efficiently in the harsh Martian environment. Given the complexity of interplanetary exploration, the success of these missions hinges on aligning numerous technological components—robotics, communication networks, environmental monitoring systems, and human-operated interfaces —into a unified operational ecosystem.

Central to this integration is understanding that Linux serves not merely as an operating system but as a foundational platform upon which diverse applications can be developed and layered. Its flexibility allows for the configuration of systems tailored to meet mission-specific needs, which is crucial for responding to the unique challenges posed by Mars. For instance, Linux can be customized to manage data processing from multiple scientific instruments, enabling seamless cross-communication between data acquisition modules and analysis tools.

Interconnectedness is a key theme in this integrated framework. Establishing exemplary communication protocols facilitated by Linux ensures that information flows seamlessly between humans on Earth and robots on Martian terrain. To this end, designing networks that can adapt to the not-so-constant communication delays and bandwidth limitations posed by the vastness of space is vital. By deploying Linux-based satellite relay systems, interplanetary networks can be formed to guarantee stable connections for data transmission and command execution, further enhancing operational efficiency.

Furthermore, the integration of Linux into robotics and autonomous systems ensures that they can operate effectively and cohesively in the Martian environment. With real-time monitoring capabilities embedded in these Linux systems, engineers can establish feedback loops that facilitate ongoing system optimization based on data collected from environmental sensors. Such adaptability is essential, allowing for decisions to be made in turbulent conditions, such as during dust storms or temperature fluctuations, without requiring immediate input from Earth-based mission control.

Human-machine interfaces also benefit from the integrated ecosystems fostered by Linux. By creating user-friendly applications that leverage Linux's resource management capabilities, mission operators can interact intuitively with the onboard systems. This collaboration enhances situational awareness, allowing astronauts and engineers to make informed decisions based on real-time data visualizations and system health reports.

In addition to operational cohesiveness, maintaining a comprehensive approach to security is paramount. As systems become increasingly interconnected, the risks associated with cyber threats also grow. Implementing robust security protocols within the Linux framework ensures that all communications and processes are safeguarded. This involves incorporating encryption and access control measures, as well as validating all inter-system communications to prevent unauthorized interference.

Another aspect of integrated systems is the emphasis on modularity and scalability. By developing modular applications that can be added or adapted as needed, mission planners can rapidly iterate and evolve functionalities to accommodate new research objectives or operational requirements. This design philosophy facilitates quick adjustments in response to unforeseen events or discoveries on Mars, promoting an agile operational stance that is essential in a dynamic exploration setting.

As we reflect on the integrated systems overview, it's imperative to recognize the broader context of how Linux is set to contribute not only to Mars missions but also to future space exploration endeavors. Whether in establishing habitats, robotic systems, communication networks, or research platforms, the integration of Linux allows for a versatile, resilient, and responsive approach to the challenges of interplanetary exploration.

In conclusion, the successful integration of Linux within Mars mission systems embodies a holistic strategy—ensuring that disparate technologies converge into a cohesive framework capable of addressing the complexities of space. By fostering this integration, we pave the way for sustainable exploration and potential human settlement in Martian territory, reinforcing Linux's vital role in shaping the future of our endeavors beyond Earth.

6.5. Long-Term Support and Maintenance Plans

In preparing for long-term support and maintenance plans for Linux-based systems that will be deployed on Mars, it is essential to consider the unique challenges that arise from operating in an unforgiving environment. Mars presents extreme conditions—ranging from significant temperature fluctuations and dust storms to cosmic radiation—that will impact both hardware and software components.

Therefore, developing a robust framework for ongoing support and maintenance is paramount for the success of interplanetary missions.

The first step in crafting effective maintenance plans involves establishing a comprehensive baseline understanding of the system's operational expectations. This entails documenting the design and configuration of Linux systems, outlining the parameters that define normal performance, and creating detailed procedures for monitoring system health. Such documentation should include various contingencies for addressing hardware failures, software errors, and environmental challenges specific to Martian conditions. This knowledge will serve as a foundation for all subsequent maintenance and support activities.

To support long-term operations, continuous monitoring capabilities must be integrated into Linux systems deployed on Mars. Utilizing sensor networks to collect and analyze data about the operational environment in real-time will enhance the system's ability to detect changes in performance or unexpected anomalies. By monitoring key metrics—such as temperature, power consumption, radiation exposure, and system responsiveness—these feedback loops allow engineers to identify potential issues early, facilitating preemptive interventions before they develop into serious failures. Given that communication delays with Earth can cause lapses in real-time responses, autonomous monitoring setups are vital.

Moreover, the implementation of remote diagnostics will enable the Linux systems to conduct periodic health checks and report performance metrics back to mission control. The capability to perform diagnostics and generate logs of system activities enhances the developers' ability to track long-term trends over the mission's duration, identifying slow degradation patterns that might signal impending failures. Hence, the ability to initiate automated recovery procedures, such as restarting failed services or re-routing operations through backup systems, can help ensure continuous functionality.

Given that human intervention will be limited on Mars, training for crew members operating Linux systems should emphasize a clear understanding of the maintenance protocols. Well-structured training materials—such as manuals, digital guides, and interactive simulations—will facilitate mastery of operational procedures, troubleshooting techniques, and emergency measures. This training will enable crew members to act quickly and efficiently, ensuring that vital systems remain functional despite the challenges posed by the Martian environment.

As part of the long-term maintenance planning, developing contingency and redundancy strategies will mitigate risks associated with unforeseen system failures. This approach may include the installation of critical systems in duplicate, allowing backup components to immediately take over when primary units fail. Implementing failover mechanisms—whereby the Linux system automatically switches to a standby unit or service—ensures continuous functionality without the need for direct human oversight, which would be particularly important in remote Martian habitats.

Software updates and patches are vital components of ongoing support and maintenance. While applying updates on Earth is straightforward, the challenge of remote application on Mars requires careful planning. Developing a structured protocol for remote software updates—comprising a secure pipeline for transmitting code, validation processes to ensure compatibility, and rollback procedures in case of failures—is essential. Enhancing automatic update systems within the Linux framework can allow patches and improvements to be applied efficiently while also enabling rollbacks if issues arise post-deployment.

In preparation for extended missions, the intrinsic adaptability of the Linux operating system allows for rapid iterations and updates. When new technologies or methods are developed—whether it be improved algorithms for navigation, data collection techniques, or advancements in environmental monitoring—having a modular architectural setup within Linux enables the integration of these innovations effectively. This approach ensures that the systems on Mars evolve in tandem with technological advancements, maintaining operational relevance throughout the mission's lifecycle.

Effective communication pathways between Mars and mission control on Earth are critical for coordinating support efforts. Establishing a dedicated communication framework that prioritizes and securely transmits vital telemetry data while permitting two-way communication reinforces the flow of information necessary for system maintenance. Utilizing Linux's networking capabilities ensures that critical updates, command requests, and performance reports can be exchanged efficiently, even when accounting for communication latency.

Periodic evaluations of the operational performance and functionality of Linux systems deployed on Mars will promote a culture of continuous improvement and adaptation. By conducting post-mission analyses and learning from past experiences, both successes and challenges can be systematically archived. This process enables engineers to reflect on what worked well and what did not and inform future mission strategies based on empirical findings.

In conclusion, developing effective long-term support and maintenance plans for Linux systems operating on Mars is a multifaceted endeavor. By focusing on continuous monitoring, remote diagnostics, contingency planning, redundancy strategies, software updates, communication frameworks, and iterative evaluations, mission planners can cultivate reliable operations that maximize the potential for successful exploration and even habitation of the Red Planet. The successful execution of these support and maintenance plans not only enhances mission resilience but ultimately serves as a stepping stone toward broader goals of interplanetary exploration.

7. Communications on Mars: Bridging the Gap with Linux

7.1. Establishing Interplanetary Networks

Establishing robust interplanetary networks for communication between Mars and Earth is one of the foremost challenges in preparing for successful missions to the Red Planet. As we embark on this ambitious journey, the need for reliable communication systems becomes distinctly apparent, driving the necessity to weave together an intricate web of technological infrastructure that utilizes Linux as a versatile operating system at its core.

A key facet of interplanetary networks lies in the deployment of satellite constellations positioned in Martian orbit. These satellites serve as communication relays, ensuring that data can seamlessly traverse the vast distances between Mars and Earth. By enabling consistent connections, these networks mitigate the potential for data loss and ensure that commands from mission control can be executed without significant delays. Implementing Linux in these satellite systems allows for real-time data processing and efficient routing of information, enhancing the overall efficacy of the communication framework.

Linux's ability to efficiently manage resources comes into play as we think about bandwidth optimization. With interplanetary communication requiring careful management of limited bandwidth, the open-source nature of Linux allows it to support various data compression techniques. These techniques enable the efficient transfer of large datasets, such as scientific measurements and imagery, while preserving the clarity and integrity of the information being transmitted. The adaptability of Linux enables developers to fine-tune these protocols to align with the specific needs and constraints posed by Martian conditions.

Another critical aspect of establishing interplanetary networks involves addressing latency, the time delay in communication resulting from the vast distance between Earth and Mars. The one-way signal delay can vary significantly—ranging from about four minutes to up to twenty-four minutes—posing challenges for real-time operations. These inherent delays necessitate the development of highly autonomous systems capable of making decisions without waiting for input from mission control.

Linux shines within this context, providing robust support for autonomous decision-making algorithms. By leveraging artificial intelligence and machine learning techniques, systems can analyze environmental data, react to immediate challenges, and optimize operations without direct human oversight. Such autonomy is essential for tasks such as navigation, where rovers must adjust their routes based on real-time sensor inputs and geographic assessments.

In creating an effective interplanetary communication network, security is a paramount consideration. The nature of space exploration means that systems are often exposed to various vulnerabilities, and ensuring the integrity of commands and data becomes crucial. By implementing Linux's robust security protocols, including encryption and access control measures, we can help safeguard against potential threats to mission systems. This ensures that all data communications between Mars and Earth remain confidential and are free from unauthorized interference.

Furthermore, Linux's modular architecture allows for flexibility in integrating additional technologies as they emerge. For instance, laser communication systems, which promise much higher data transfer rates than traditional radio communications, could be deployed in future missions. This adaptability means that the underlying Linux operating system can accommodate such advancements swiftly, thereby future-proofing the interplanetary network against evolving communication technologies.

In addition to interplanetary communication, systems must be established for remote access and monitoring of all operations on Mars. With limited opportunities for hands-on intervention from Earth, mission control must have the ability to monitor telemetry and status reports from Martian systems effectively. Using Linux-based applications tailored for remote data management, we can ensure that mission control is well-informed about system performance and can execute commands or adjustments as necessary. This fosters an environment where operators can act proactively to address any emerging challenges.

The feedback mechanisms designed within Linux systems will allow for iterative learning from mission performance, enabling refinements in both communication processes and network resilience. They facilitate a broader understanding of how systems interact within the Martian environment, providing insights that can enhance future missions as well.

In summary, establishing interplanetary networks for Mars requires meticulous planning and the integration of robust technologies tailored for the unique challenges of deep-space communication. Harnessing Linux's capabilities allows us to mitigate communication delays through autonomous systems, optimize bandwidth, ensure secure data transmission, and adapt to emerging technologies. As we lay the groundwork for a successful communications framework, it is crucial to remember that interconnected, resilient systems are fundamental to the success of our missions on Mars—ultimately bridging the vast distance between two worlds.

7.2. Delays and Latency Issues

Delays and latency issues represent a significant challenge in the realm of interplanetary communication, particularly as we seek to explore and eventually inhabit Mars. The inherent distances between Earth and Mars mean that any communication, whether data transmission or command execution, is subject to unavoidable delays caused by the speed of light. Addressing these challenges requires a combination of advanced technology, strategic system design, and operational pragmatism.

First, it is essential to grasp the basic parameters of this issue. The time it takes for radio signals to travel between Earth and Mars can vary significantly based on their respective positions in their orbits. The one-way delay can range from approximately 4 minutes to 24 minutes. This latency fundamentally alters the dynamics of communication, particularly concerning commands requiring real-time execution, such as navigation adjustments for rovers moving across Martian terrain. As a result, operators on Earth cannot afford to rely solely on direct control—these delays necessitate an autonomous operational capacity for any systems deployed on Mars.

In response to these challenges, Linux-based systems deployed on Mars must be designed with a focus on autonomy. Rovers that rely on swift decision-making—whether avoiding obstacles or adjusting to unexpected environmental changes—must be operated through algorithms that enable independent functioning. Machine learning and artificial intelligence capabilities implemented within the Linux framework can facilitate this level of sophistication. By utilizing real-time sensor data and stored knowledge of the terrain, these systems can make informed decisions without the need for human input, thereby navigating the challenges of the Martian environment effectively.

One pivotal aspect of minimizing the impact of delays is the implementation of planning algorithms and prediction models within the Linux operating systems of Martian systems. These algorithms can analyze historical data related to Earth-Mars communications, adapting methodologies to preemptively account for systemic latency. For instance, mission planners can develop protocols that allow rovers to schedule activities based on expected communication windows with mission control. As a result, rather than waiting for a command to act, the rovers can autonomously engage in simple tasks—like repositioning or data collection—based on their programmed objectives.

Another strategic solution involves the establishment of pre-set commands that can function effectively without real-time oversight. During the planning phase of a mission, sets of scripts can be loaded into Linux systems on rovers, allowing them to conduct scheduled tasks autonomously. This could include instructions for drilling into Martian soil, scientific experiments, or data gathering—all programmed to execute without awaiting real-time confirmations from Earth. Such orchestration can utilize the unique parameters of Mars' environment to optimize mission output despite the communication hurdles.

Moreover, utilizing advanced data compression techniques to optimize bandwidth usage further complements strategies addressing latency. In a situation where signal delays complicate communication logistics, efficient data management becomes paramount. Linux can serve as a platform for sophisticated compression algorithms that condense data outputs into manageable packets before being transmitted to Earth. This ensures that mission-critical information is relayed efficiently, minimizing the time required to send large files such as high-resolution images or extensive datasets.

Redundancy also plays a critical role in mitigating the impacts of communication delays. By deploying multiple communication pathways—such as satellite relays around Mars operating alongside direct linkages to Earth—mission planners can create backup options that assure resilience even when primary communications are affected. Linux's modular architecture allows for the flexibility needed to implement these redundant systems effectively. When a failure occurs in one communication pathway, alternative routing options ensure continuity of operations, enabling ongoing data flow.

Additionally, providing interfaces for remote access and monitoring is essential for managing the effects of latency. Linux-based systems can maintain vital health metrics that allow Earth-based operators to observe performance, diagnose faults, and propose adjustments seamlessly. Even amidst communication delays, the capacity to monitor system status in real time can lead to more informed decisions about system operations—an essential capability for maintaining optimal functionality in challenging environments.

Lastly, ongoing research into improving interplanetary communication technologies can help alleviate the challenges posed by delays and latency. Innovations in laser communication systems, for example, promise significantly higher data transfer rates compared to traditional radio systems. By ensuring that Linux systems are compatible with emerging communication technologies, mission planners can support the evolution of interplanetary communication methods, eventually transitioning to these faster networks as they are developed.

In summary, managing delays and latency issues is critical for the success of Martian missions that rely on Linux systems. By implementing autonomous functionalities, developing future-proof communication strategies, and optimizing data transmission, we can minimize the inherent delays associated with interplanetary communication. With each innovation, we bring humanity one step closer to not just exploring but sustaining life on Mars, firmly bridging the gap between two worlds across the vast void of space.

7.3. Remote Access and Monitoring

Remote access and monitoring are critical components in the operation of systems deployed on Mars, enabling missions to run efficiently despite the challenges posed by the planet's harsh environment and the inherent communication delays with Earth. The implementation of effective remote access and monitoring protocols requires leveraging Linux as a flexible operating system capable of adapting to various circumstances and enabling real-time data management and oversight.

The design of remote access systems begins with a clear understanding of the communication architecture necessary for interplanetary operations. Given the significant latency that characterizes Mars-Earth interactions, establishing reliable and secure communication channels is paramount. Linux-based systems can incorporate a variety of networking protocols and frameworks that facilitate the seamless transmission of signals between Martian rovers, landers, and orbital satellites. These protocols must be efficient, as they will need to handle high volumes of data while navigating the challenges posed by communication delays.

One of the primary objectives of remote access is to enable mission control on Earth to monitor the health and status of all systems deployed on Mars. This monitoring can include the status of scientific instruments, energy consumption metrics, environmental levels (such as temperature and radiation), and operational performance. By integrating comprehensive telemetry tools into the Linux environment used on Mars, operators can receive detailed reports that ensure all systems are functioning within expected parameters. Such continuous oversight can identify abnormal behaviors, allowing for proactive measures to address potential issues before they become significant problems.

Real-time monitoring in Linux also enhances the safety and reliability of Martian operations. Health monitoring applications can track each system's vital signs and provide alerts in the event that thresholds are breached. For example, if a rover's temperature exceeds safety limits due to extreme Martian conditions, automated responses can kick in that adjust operational parameters or activate cooling systems. Remote access to operational dashboards—affording both graphical and textual representations of performance metrics—equips mission teams with instant visibility into system health, enabling informed decision-making even during periods of latency.

Security is another essential component to consider when establishing remote access and monitoring systems on Mars. Given the vulnerability of systems susceptible to unauthorized access, implementing robust security protocols is vital to ensure the integrity of communications. Utilizing Linux's built-in security features, such as encryption and access control, safeguards data exchange between Martian systems and Earth-based mission control. Two-factor authentication mechanisms for remote access can provide an additional security layer to protect sensitive operations. Encrypting transmissions ensures that data remains confidential and cannot be intercepted or manipulated during transit.

Collaboration in remote monitoring is also vital. By utilizing Linux's open-source nature, engineers and scientists from various space agencies can contribute to the development of tools and applications that support remote access and monitoring. This collaborative approach can lead to enhanced capabilities, as diverse teams bring unique perspectives and expertise to the challenge of monitoring Martian systems effectively. Custom software applications, tailored for specific scientific experiments or operational tasks, can be developed collaboratively, enriching the overall monitoring ecosystem.

Implementing remote access systems also presents opportunities for automation. By programming Linux environments to perform routine monitoring tasks autonomously, mission control can optimize system management without needing continuous human intervention. Scripts and procedures can be designed to run diagnostic tests at predefined intervals, data logging can occur automatically, and alerts generated in the event of any irregularities. Such automation not only eases the workload for mission control personnel but also enhances overall operational efficiency in unpredictable environments.

Moreover, the integration of advanced data analytics and machine learning algorithms within the Linux framework can elevate remote monitoring capabilities. These technologies can analyze the collected telemetry data to detect trends, predict failures, and discover insights that may not be readily apparent through manual monitoring. By utilizing AI-driven analytics, system performance can be optimized continuously in response to changing conditions within the Martian atmosphere—ranging from dust accumulation and temperature shifts to power fluctuations due to solar exposure.

Ultimately, the approach to remote access and monitoring aligns with the larger overarching goal of sustaining operations on Mars over the long term. By ensuring that robust systems are in place to observe and respond to the dynamic Martian environment while permitting mission control to engage efficiently with deployed technologies, space exploration efforts can realize their full potential. Preparing for the unknowns of the Martian landscape requires a commitment to resilience, adaptability, and collaboration, and Linux, with its plethora of features and community support, provides an ideal platform to meet these challenges.

In conclusion, establishing effective remote access and monitoring systems for Mars missions prepares us to explore the Red Planet more intelligently and safely. By prioritizing communication architecture, facilitating real-time monitoring, implementing robust security protocols, and leveraging collaboration and automation, we create an ecosystem that enables Linux systems to thrive on Mars, ultimately paving the way for continuous exploration and discovery in this extraordinary new frontier.

7.4. Security Protocols in Communications

In the expansive endeavor of space exploration, securing communications is an essential element for successful missions, particularly those targeting Mars. As we prepare for the embodiment of these ambitious goals, the implementation of robust security protocols in communication processes becomes a paramount focus. This section will explore the critical need for secure communication practices within the context of open environments that characterize space missions, emphasizing the integration of Linux systems in fostering reliable, resilient, and secure communication frameworks.

The first aspect of security in communication on Mars involves understanding the vulnerabilities inherent in data transmission across long distances. The vast gap between Earth and Mars is not just a geographical challenge but also a technological one, leading to potential disruptions and unauthorized interceptions that can jeopardize mission integrity. As signals relay through an array of satellite networks, it becomes vital to ensure that security measures are in place throughout the communication chain, protecting sensitive data from malicious actors and environmental disruptions alike.

Linux, as an open-source operating system, lends itself excellently to building these secure communication frameworks due to its flexible architecture. Coupled with the developer community's collaborative spirit, Linux can adapt and integrate cutting-edge security protocols to ensure all communication channels remain secure and resilient. For instance, utilizing protocols such as Secure Socket Layer (SSL) or Transport Layer Security (TLS) ensures that all transmitted data between Mars-based and Earth-based systems is encrypted, rendering intercepted communications unreadable. Given the autonomy required by Martian systems, adopting end-to-end encryption methods is essential to maintain the confidentiality of command instructions and transmitted scientific data.

Additionally, implementing robust authentication measures can significantly bolster communication security. This entails employing multi-factor authentication systems for accessing critical applications or command pathways within the Linux environment, ensuring that only authorized personnel have the ability to send commands or receive data from Mars. Developers can construct authentication layers that verify user identities through various methods—ranging from password protection to biometric verification—strengthening defenses against potential breaches.

The principle of minimizing the attack surface is critical in addressing vulnerabilities in Mars communications. By limiting the number of access points and employing firewall configurations within the Linux environment, mission planners can restrict unauthorized access to mission systems. Utilizing technologies such as software-defined networking (SDN) ensures that the communication pathways are adaptable, allowing for rapid adjustments in firewall rules or access control lists in response to identified threats or unanticipated risks.

Establishing redundancy in communication pathways further contributes to enhancing resilience against communication failures or interruptions. Deploying multiple satellites or communication channels ensures that if one route experiences issues or becomes compromised, operations remain unaffected. Linux's modular framework allows for the seamless integration of these redundancy protocols, automatically switching to backup systems as needed. This characteristic reflects the importance of designing robust backup communication systems that emphasize resilience while concurrently maintaining mission objectives across various Martian activities.

Moreover, employing real-time logging and monitoring functions within Linux is crucial for detecting anomalies in communication that could signal security breaches. By maintaining detailed logs of all data transmissions and receiving logs, engineers can analyze communication patterns and identify inconsistencies that may point to unauthorized interception or corruption. This capability allows for proactive measures to engage cutting-edge intrusion detection systems capable of reacting swiftly to identified threats.

As a part of strategic planning, it is essential to train all personnel involved in Martian missions about the significance of communication security. Education on identifying phishing attacks, understanding the importance of proper data management, and enforcing secure operational protocols fortifies the overall security posture of the mission. Awareness training empowers mission personnel to recognize potential threats and implement mitigation strategies, fostering a culture of security consciousness across all stages of mission planning and execution.

Finally, collaboration with international partners in the domain of space exploration invites opportunities to share best practices in securing communications. Engaging with global space agencies fosters an exchange of methodologies, technologies, and tools that enhance security measures across all interconnected systems. These partnerships can promote the joint development of communication protocols designed explicitly for the complexities of space environments, ensuring that our interplanetary communication strategies remain steadfast against the myriad of challenges posed by cybersecurity threats.

In conclusion, implementing security protocols in communications for Mars missions facilitated by Linux systems stands as a foundational pillar to ensuring mission success. Through the adoption of robust encryption methods, authentication measures, minimized attack surfaces, redundancy in communication pathways, comprehensive monitoring capabilities, personnel training, and global collaborations, we can effectively mitigate potential risks. As we venture further into the cosmos, the commitment to securing communications will play a transformative role in actualizing our aspirations for Martian exploration and paving the way for humanity's enduring presence on the Red Planet and beyond.

7.5. Data Retrieval and Processing

Data retrieval and processing are essential elements for the success of any Martian mission, particularly within the context of remote operations where hundreds of millions of kilometers pose a significant challenge in terms of communication latency and data management. As we prepare to implement Linux systems on Mars, it is crucial to establish robust methodologies and technologies that ensure timely and efficient data acquisition, storage, transmission, and analysis in the face of the unique challenges presented by this alien environment.

The first consideration in effective data retrieval on Mars lies in the design and implementation of sophisticated sensors and instruments capable of capturing a wide array of environmental metrics. From geological samples to atmospheric readings, these instruments generate large volumes of data that must be accurately collected and managed. Linux-based systems provide the necessary platform for integrating these diverse data streams, allowing for seamless and organized retrieval processes. Real-time processing capabilities ensure that critical data is accessible at the moment of collection, facilitating immediate assessment and utilization.

Central to efficient data retrieval is the architecture of the data management system. Utilizing Linux's flexibility, data repositories can be established that are optimized for the specific requirements of Martian operations. These repositories must be designed to handle high volumes of scientific data, necessitating the use of high-performance file systems capable of quick data input and retrieval cycles. Technologies such as the ext4 file system allow for effective handling of large datasets, ensuring data integrity and availability under the demanding conditions on Mars.

Data compression techniques are also crucial in optimizing the limited storage and bandwidth available on Martian missions. By employing advanced compression algorithms integrated within the Linux environment, large datasets can be reduced in size without compromising essential information. This is especially important when considering the constraints of interplanetary communication, where data packets transmitted to Earth must be as small as possible. Efficiently formatted packets ensure that mission-critical information can be transmitted within the limited bandwidth, enhancing the reliability of data transfer while minimizing transmission times.

Following data retrieval, processing needs are equally fundamental for deriving valuable insights from the collected information. Here, the powerful computational capabilities provided by Linux come to the forefront. Advanced data analysis tools and machine learning algorithms can be implemented to process and interpret the data collected by Martian instruments. For instance, geological data can be analyzed using pattern recognition algorithms to identify mineral compositions, while atmospheric readings can be assessed to model weather patterns or potential dust storms. These analytics enhance scientific understanding while reducing the reliance on Earth-based teams to conduct real-time analyses.

Moreover, the integration of artificial intelligence within Linux systems bolsters the efficiency of data processing. Real-time decision-making algorithms can parse collected data and suggest autonomous actions based on predefined thresholds or anomalies detected in the environmental readings. For instance, if a rover identifies high radiation levels nearing its operational threshold, AI-driven protocols can trigger pre-emptive actions—such as returning to shelter or altering power consumption to avoid damage.

Given that communication with Earth involves latency ranging from a few minutes to over twenty minutes, effective data storage and transmission protocols must be established. This is where local data processing capabilities become integral. By conducting preliminary data assessments onboard, systems can prioritize what information is sent back to Earth based on scientific importance, urgency, and available bandwidth. Hence, not all collected data will need immediate transmission, allowing the Linux-based systems to act autonomously and selectively send only the most pertinent information.

Backup and redundancy protocols also play a critical role in data management on Mars. Systems must be designed to duplicate critical datasets, ensuring that no essential information is lost in the event of hardware failures or corruption. The inherent reliability of the Linux platform supports these redundancy measures through its ability to manage multiple instances of essential applications, providing alternative access points in case primary pathways fail.

Finally, the establishment of a secure data transmission framework is essential to safeguard the integrity of information exchanged between Martian systems and Earth. With the risks posed by potential interference or unauthorized access, Linux's robust security frameworks must be employed to encrypt transmitted data and authenticate access to mission-critical components. This ensures that scientific findings and operational data remain secure and intact during communication.

In summary, the intricacies of data retrieval and processing on Mars require a multifaceted approach that effectively utilizes the capabilities of Linux systems. By optimizing data management architectures, employing sophisticated data analysis algorithms, ensuring the integrity and security of data, and adapting to the unique Martian environment, we can establish a robust framework that supports the exploration and study of the Red Planet. This carefully coordinated strategy will not only maximize the potential for scientific discovery but also enhance the overall effectiveness and resilience of missions as we take significant steps toward humanity's future on Mars.

8. Ensuring Survival: Systems Ecology and Sustainability

8.1. Building Sustainable Habitats with Technology

Building sustainable habitats on Mars is an ambitious endeavor that requires innovative approaches to technology as we prepare for long-term human presence on the planet. These habitats must address extreme environmental conditions, provide life support, and maximize resource efficiency, all while ensuring the safety and wellbeing of their occupants. By integrating technology and leveraging the capabilities of Linux-based systems, we can develop smart habitats that support human life on Mars sustainably and efficiently.

The design of Martian habitats must focus on protecting inhabitants from the harsh environmental conditions on Mars, including extreme temperatures, radiation, and dust storms. Insulation and thermal management systems become critical, ensuring that habitats remain habitable despite the wide temperature fluctuations that can occur from day to night. Utilizing Linux, we can integrate advanced climate control systems capable of automating temperature regulation, managing HVAC (heating, ventilation, and air conditioning) functions based on real-time data from internal and external sensors. This capability ensures that the interior climate remains stable, providing comfort and safety for those residing within.

In addition to temperature management, the habitat design must include effective shielding against cosmic radiation. Mars lacks a protective magnetic field and has a thin atmosphere that offers minimal protection from solar and cosmic radiation. Strategic implementation of radiation-hardened materials within the habitat structure can be integrated into the design with Linux-based systems programmed to monitor radiation levels continuously. Adaptations might include deploying movable shielding—such as retractable panels or specific areas designated as shielded zones—allowing residents to access outdoor environments while minimizing radiation exposure during solar events.

An essential aspect of sustainable habitats is the efficient management of resources, such as food, water, and energy. In a closed-loop ecological system, implementing advanced resource management technologies ensures that every element is utilized effectively. This approach includes utilizing hydroponics or aeroponics for food production, allowing for crops to be grown without soil, thus maximizing space and minimizing the need for extensive terrestrial supplies. Linux-based control systems can monitor plant growth conditions, adjusting variables such as light, nutrients, and humidity in real-time to ensure optimal yields from minimal resource input.

Water is another key element for sustainability on Mars. There are signs that water ice exists beneath the Martian surface, and future habitats will need to incorporate systems to extract, purify, and recycle water for human consumption and agricultural use. Implementing water recycling technologies—similar to those used aboard the International Space Station—within the habitat design will allow for the filtration and purification of wastewater. Linux systems can manage these processes autonomously, ensuring that water quality is continuously monitored while adjusting treatments based on real-time data analytics.

Energy management is paramount in sustainable habitats, where reliance on solar energy is likely to play a significant role. Martian habitats must incorporate solar panels optimized for performance under varying light conditions, particularly considering the frequent dust storms that can obscure sunlight. Leveraging the capabilities of Linux, energy management systems can optimize solar energy collection by utilizing algorithms to adjust panel angles for maximum exposure. Moreover, these systems can monitor energy usage within the habitat, dynamically allocating resources to essential functions while conserving power for non-critical systems.

Waste management is another crucial component of habitat sustainability, requiring protocols to minimize waste production while recycling usable materials. Linux-based systems can facilitate efficient waste sorting and processing—transforming organic waste into compost for use in agricultural systems or repurposing materials for construction and repairs. By employing waste-to-energy techniques, habitats can convert non-recyclable waste into usable energy, supporting a closed-loop ecosystem that minimizes resource depletion and upholds ecological balance.

Creating a centralized monitoring and control system through a Linux-based interface can facilitate the seamless operation of various habitat functions, allowing occupants to manage all aspects of their living environment from a single point of control. Remote access capabilities will give mission control on Earth insights into habitat conditions, performance metrics, and system health data, offering proactive support for ongoing operations. Cloud-based solutions could allow for data analysis, while user-friendly interfaces enable habitation team members to interact with automated systems easily.

In establishing sustainable habitats on Mars, it is essential to iterate upon designs based on continuous evaluation and feedback. Deploying prototypes and conducting simulations of operational systems can yield invaluable insights into the effectiveness of various technologies and designs before actual implementation. The iterative design process, facilitated by Linux, allows for quick adaptations based on real-life findings to refine habitats and ensure their sustainability.

In conclusion, building sustainable habitats on Mars requires a multifaceted approach that encompasses comprehensive environmental management, resource optimization, technological integration, and collaborative decision-making. Through the application of Linux-based systems, we can ensure that these habitats not only support human life but also foster a sustainable presence in a challenging extraterrestrial environment. As we move forward with our endeavors in Martian exploration, the commitment to sustainability will stand as a cornerstone of our efforts, shaping the future of human existence beyond our home planet.

8.2. Resource Management Systems

Resource management systems are pivotal in the context of Martian missions, particularly as we strive to establish sustainable human presence on another planet. As we prepare to harness our technological capabilities, understanding how to efficiently manage resources through the lens of Linux becomes essential for success. The unique challenges posed by the Martian environment—spanning extreme temperatures, limited accessibility to in-situ resources, and the complexities of closed-loop ecological systems—demand innovative approaches rooted in intelligent design and operational efficiency.

At the heart of effective resource management is the need for comprehensive monitoring and optimization of all available materials—be it energy, water, food, or construction resources. Linux, with its robust ecosystem of applications and outstanding adaptability, serves as an ideal platform to coordinate these diverse management functions. The open-source nature of Linux also enhances the ability to customize the operating system, tailoring individual applications to specific mission goals while allowing scientists and engineers to modify and improve functionalities in real-time.

One crucial aspect of resource management involves energy optimization. With sustainable habitats relying on renewable energy sources such as solar power, the efficiency of energy consumption becomes paramount. Linux-based systems can integrate advanced energy management algorithms that monitor, control, and optimize energy distribution throughout the habitat. This includes intelligent scheduling of energy-intensive tasks during peak solar collection periods, predictive analytics to forecast potential energy shortages, and real-time adjustments to ensure power is allocated to critical functions first—such as life support systems and scientific operations.

Water management presents another critical focus area. Mars holds considerable potential for water resource utilization, particularly in accessing subsurface ice and recycling wastewater. A sophisticated resource management system deployed on Linux can automate the processes of water extraction, purification, and recycling—enabling closed-loop water systems to operate efficiently. Pressure sensors, valves, and filters can be integrated into the Linux environment for real-time monitoring. This includes tracking water quality and availability, allowing occupants to understand their consumption patterns while adjusting as required to ensure sustainability.

The necessity of effective waste management also forms the backbone of successful resource management systems. As habitats on Mars will operate in closed-loop systems, waste must be minimized, reused, or repurposed whenever possible. Linux systems can be utilized to dynamically categorize and process waste streams, using classification algorithms to sort materials for recycling, composting, or incineration as appropriate. This integration of waste processing technologies ensures that the habitat maintains a clean and sustainable environment, supporting long-term human habitation by preventing the accumulation of waste that could compromise living conditions.

Agricultural technology is an integral part of resource management on Mars, facilitating food production in controlled environments. Linux-based systems can manage hydroponic or aeroponic growing systems, allowing for the optimal growth of crops with minimal water and space. These systems can monitor vital parameters such as nutrient levels, pH balance, and growth rates, providing automated adjustments to support optimal agricultural production. This ability to tailor food production systems efficiently aligns with the overarching goal of self-sufficiency, essential for sustainable living in Martian habitats.

Beyond energy, water, waste, and food, building materials and construction resources require effective management as well. Future missions will likely focus on utilizing in-situ resource utilization (ISRU) methods to convert Martian materials into construction supplies. Developing a Linux-based resource management system capable of modeling various geological features and assessing the viability of local materials can streamline the construction process. This system can assist mission planners in determining which resources can be easily and safely extracted and utilized for building habitats and infrastructure, minimizing dependence on Earth-supplied materials.

Furthermore, creating an interconnected resource management system enables synergy among various subsystems. With all components managed through a Linux architecture, data from energy consumption, water usage, food production, and construction resources can be integrated. This holistic view of resource availability allows for advanced assessments and decision-making, creating a responsive operational environment—identifying potential bottlenecks and adjusting processes preemptively to support mission goals.

Training is essential in effectively implementing resource management systems, ensuring that crews aboard Martian habitats understand how to use the Linux-based technologies designed for their day-to-day operations. Comprehensive training programs can facilitate simulated environments, allowing crew members to practice critical functions, collaborate seamlessly, and become accustomed to automated processes and decision-making systems.

In conclusion, resource management systems represent a vital element of planning for sustainable habitats on Mars. By leveraging Linux's capabilities, we can design intelligent systems that monitor, optimize, and support the efficient consumption of resources critical for human survival. This holistic, integrated approach not only enhances mission reliability and resilience but also paves the way for self-sustaining ecosystems capable of sustaining human life in the extremes of outer space, transforming our aspirations for Martian exploration into reality.

8.3. Agricultural Technology and Cultivation

As humanity aims to establish a sustainable presence on Mars, agricultural technology and cultivation will play a pivotal role in ensuring food security for long-term missions. Effective use of technology for agricultural purposes will not only enable food production but also create a self-sustaining ecosystem within Martian habitats. This approach integrates innovative techniques, resource management, and the adaptability of Linux-based systems to optimize cultivation in the challenging Martian environment.

To begin with, establishing a controlled agricultural environment is crucial. Given Mars' harsh conditions—such as low atmospheric pressure, extreme temperatures, and limited sunlight during dust storms—creating an optimal growing environment will require precision technology and monitoring systems. The use of hydroponics or aeroponics allows for efficient utilization of water and space, reducing the reliance on traditional soil-based growing methods. These soilless systems can be managed by Linux-based control units that monitor nutrient delivery, pH levels, and environmental conditions, ensuring that crops receive optimal growth conditions.

The customization of Linux to interface with sensors and automation systems within hydroponic or aeroponic environments is essential. Temperature, humidity, and CO_2 levels can be continuously monitored and adjusted by automated systems that communicate through the Linux interface. For instance, if CO_2 levels drop below optimal levels, Linux systems can trigger CO_2 infusion to enhance photosynthesis, thereby maximizing crop yields. Similarly, monitoring systems can detect any fluctuations in temperature, initiating heating or cooling responses to maintain stability.

Moreover, given the limited availability of water on Mars, implementing closed-loop water systems is vital. Linux systems can facilitate water recycling by collecting excess moisture through condensation, capturing it for reuse in the agricultural system. Monitoring the water cycle closely within the habitat and ensuring that all systems—be it for irrigation, plant growth, or crew consumption—are interconnected allows for optimal water management. This holistic approach ensures minimal waste and maximizes the efficiency of available resources.

The cultivation process will also benefit significantly from the integration of machine learning and artificial intelligence within Linux-controlled environments. Predictive analytics can analyze historical performance data from crop cycles to optimize growth parameters dynamically. For example, machine learning algorithms can ascertain which plant species thrive best in the Martian environment by analyzing growth patterns, nutrient uptake, and environmental responses. By employing these insights, mission planners can select crops suited for cultivation, enhancing food production and resource utilization.

Furthermore, it is essential to consider the seasonal variations on Mars and their potential effects on crop growth. The planet experiences significant axial tilt and varying periods of sunlight duration which can impact the growing cycle. Utilizing Linux systems equipped with smart algorithms can adaptively control light exposure to simulate optimal conditions for plant growth throughout the Martian sol (day). By mimicking the natural photoperiod experienced on Earth, crops can be cultivated successfully despite Mars' unique solar patterns.

An additional layer of resilience involves integrating modularity into the agricultural systems. Utilizing Linux allows for the implementation of modular components such that specific aspects of cultivation can be upgraded or modified without the need for a complete system overhaul. For example, if advancements in LED lighting technology emerge, new lighting systems can be introduced without disrupting the efficient operation of hydroponic or sensor networks already in place. This adaptability supports continuous improvement based on emerging technologies or new scientific insights relevant to Martian agriculture.

Varying the types of crops cultivated is also crucial for nutrition and agricultural sustainability. Diversifying plant species grown helps ensure that the crew receives necessary vitamins and nutrients while reducing the risks associated with monoculture systems. Incorporating an array of edible plants, including grains, vegetables, and fruits, requires careful planning and management. Leveraging Linux for crop rotation and planning protocols ensures that nutrient depletion is managed effectively, maintaining soil health and supporting a balanced diet for crew members.

Finally, successful operation of agricultural technologies relies upon effective training programs for crew members who will manage these systems. Training should encompass all relevant aspects of operating Linux-based agricultural controls, from understanding sensor data to operating automation protocols. By ensuring that crew members are well-versed in system management, they can quickly address any issues that arise, fostering confidence and proficiency in day-to-day operations.

In conclusion, integrating agricultural technology and cultivation systems within the context of Martian exploration is fundamental for establishing sustainable habitats on the planet. Through the effective utilization of Linux-based systems, hydroponics, AI-driven predictive analytics, and modular design, we can create resilient agricultural ecosystems capable of supporting human life on Mars. This approach not only addresses food security but fosters a vision of self-sustainability that aligns with humanity's broader goals of interplanetary colonization. As we look to the future, the principles of sustainable cultivation will play a vital role in enabling humanity's journey beyond Earth, ensuring that we can thrive on distant worlds.

8.4. Water and Waste Systems

Water and waste systems are critical components for the success of Martian missions, particularly as we strive to create sustainable habitats and support human life on the planet. Efficient management of both water resources and waste products will be essential to ensure that missions can operate effectively over extended periods. By leveraging advanced technology, especially Linux-based systems, we can create robust frameworks for controlling water use and waste processing that align with the unique challenges presented by the Martian environment.

The management of water on Mars begins with the understanding of its limited availability and the necessity for sustainability. While evidence suggests the presence of water ice beneath the surface, access to this resource will require innovative extraction techniques. Linux systems can be implemented to control automated drilling and extraction systems, collecting subsurface ice and converting it into usable liquid water through methods like heating or melting. Such deployments will rely on real-time data captured by sensors that monitor temperature, pressure, and the integrity of extraction mechanisms. By integrating these datasets, Linux can ensure effective decision-making during the extraction process, optimizing operations and resource management.

Once water is extracted, its purification and recycling will be paramount to maintaining a closed-loop ecosystem. Water used within habitats must be treated to ensure it is free from contaminants, supporting human health and safety. Utilizing Linux, we can design sophisticated water filtration and purification processes that automate chemical treatments and monitor water quality. In real-time, these systems can detect contaminants and adjust purification protocols accordingly, utilizing feedback mechanisms to ensure that only safe, potable water is consumed.

Additionally, the habitat design must account for the recycling of wastewater. Closed-loop water systems that treat greywater from communal activities and urine collection will be necessary for sustainability. Linux systems can manage these operations, controlling the filtration, biological treatment, and filtration processes required to reclaim water. By implementing monitoring mechanisms that assess water recovery efficiency, the system can continually improve treatment processes to maximize water reuse.

Waste management is another critical aspect that works in tandem with water systems. Martian habitats will produce various waste streams, including organic waste from food production and human waste, necessitating efficient disposal and recycling processes. Linux can facilitate the development of waste sorting and processing systems to minimize the ecological footprint of missions. Through intelligent waste management controls, materials can be categorized and repurposed—organic waste can be composted for agricultural use, while plastics might be recycled into useful construction materials.

Implementing a waste-to-energy system could also provide significant benefits by converting waste products into usable energy or fuel. Utilizing pyrolysis or anaerobic digestion, Linux-controlled systems can efficiently process waste, producing biogas that could be harnessed to power habitat systems or vehicles. This integration of waste management with energy production supports both sustainability and operational efficiency, aligning with the broader goals of maintaining life on Mars.

Integration and automation are key components of managing water and waste systems effectively. A centralized Linux-based control system allows for the streamlined coordination of various operations, enabling seamless communication between water purification units, recycling systems, and waste processing facilities. By creating an interconnected architecture, real-time data flow ensures that all systems can respond adaptively to changing conditions or resource availability.

Moreover, the training of crew members operating these systems is essential for their effective management. Ensuring that personnel are well-versed in the processes, protocols, and troubleshooting techniques associated with these water and waste systems will empower them to manage daily operations competently. Utilization of Linux-based training simulators can replicate real scenarios, allowing crew members to gain hands-on experience in a controlled environment.

In conclusion, the effective management of water and waste systems will be integral to the success of Martian missions. By harnessing the versatility and adaptability of Linux, we can build robust frameworks capable of extracting, purifying, recycling, and managing water and waste sustainably. This comprehensive approach not only ensures the safety and well-being of crew members but also fosters ecological resilience, paving the way for future exploration and potential colonization of Mars.

8.5. Solar Energy Utilization with Linux Systems

In the context of harnessing solar energy for Martian missions, the integration of Linux-based systems is not merely advantageous but essential. The unique challenges presented by the Martian environment, characterized by its thin atmosphere, varied solar exposure, and extreme temperature fluctuations, make it imperative that we fully optimize solar energy utilization to ensure the sustainability of long-term missions.

First and foremost, effective solar energy management requires a comprehensive understanding of the specific operational parameters of Martian solar panels. The comparatively lower solar irradiance reaching Mars—approximately 60% of that on Earth—means that solar collectors must be designed to maximize efficiency, especially during periods of suboptimal sunlight, such as during dust storms or at higher latitudes. Linux, with its renowned flexibility, can be programmed to control solar panel adjustments based on real-time environmental data, allowing panels to track the sun's position throughout the Martian day. This capability enhances energy capture, ensuring that solar panels are consistently oriented for optimal exposure.

Additionally, given the frequently dusty and windy conditions on Mars, the need for maintenance becomes critical. Dust accumulation can significantly reduce solar panel efficiency, necessitating regular cleaning. Linux can manage automated cleaning mechanisms, acting on sensor data that monitors the panels for dust levels and performance metrics. By deploying robotic arms or utilizing vibration-assisted cleaning systems engineered within a Linux framework, habitats can ensure continuous optimal performance of solar energy systems without requiring human intervention, thereby alleviating staff from routine maintenance tasks.

Once solar energy is harvested, the next challenge involves effective energy storage and distribution. Energy management systems built on Linux can monitor power generation and usage in real-time, dynamically allocating resources based on demand. Implementations may include smart grid technologies that optimize energy flow within habitats, ensuring that critical systems—such as life support and scientific research operations—receive the necessary power while allowing for energy conservation strategies during low production periods. For example, during Martian nights, when solar panels cannot provide energy, Linux-based systems can engage backup batteries or initiate energy-saving protocols to prioritize key systems.

The potential overlap with artificial intelligence (AI) marks a further enhancement to solar energy management. By integrating machine learning algorithms driven by Linux, solar energy systems can learn from historical performance data to refine their response to variable conditions continually. For instance, predicting patterns such as dust storm occurrences or assessing solar energy production based on seasonal variations could enable preemptive adjustments—like temporarily shifting the orientation of solar panels.

Moreover, as we scale to larger habitats or networks of rovers, the ability to manage decentralized solar energy systems becomes paramount. Linux can efficiently establish distributed energy management models that connect multiple solar installations and storage facilities. This interconnected architecture ensures that energy can be shared across various systems—maximizing resource utilization and supporting interdependent operations on Mars. With a Linux foundation, habitats can dynamically distribute energy between inhabitants and operational needs, promoting efficiency and resilience in energy usage.

Integration with other resource management systems also strengthens the potential for optimized solar energy utilization. For example, cross-referencing solar energy data with water and waste management metrics can lead to innovative approaches for resource conservation. If energy production dips, users could be alerted to temporarily reduce water consumption or other energy-intensive operations to maintain equilibrium.

Finally, establishing robust communication pathways allows for insights and updates to be shared with mission control on Earth. A Linux-based energy management system can automate data reporting concerning energy production, storage status, and overall efficiency, providing researchers and engineers with insights to refine and enhance solar energy strategies. These updates could guide mission control in suggesting operational tweaks based on performance data, fostering an ongoing feedback loop that enhances the solar energy strategy over time.

In conclusion, the use of Linux systems for solar energy utilization on Mars promises to optimize the energy management necessary for sustaining human presence on the Red Planet. Through robust automation, intelligent monitoring, and efficient communication, we can harness the potential of solar energy to support sustained operations for future Martian missions. By continuously refining these systems in coordination with the unique Martian environment, we set a formidable foundation for long-term human exploration of Mars and beyond.

9. AI and Autonomous Systems in Martian Missions

9.1. The Role of AI in Space Exploration

In the vast expanse of the universe, artificial intelligence (AI) is becoming an indispensable ally in our quest for space exploration and the establishment of human presence beyond Earth. As we venture further into the cosmos, particularly with ambitious plans for Mars, the role of AI expands in transforming how we navigate, analyze, and interact with our extraterrestrial environments. This exploration into the role of AI illustrates its potential to enhance the efficiency and effectiveness of our missions, ensuring that we make data-driven decisions while also automating complex tasks that would be unmanageable in their entirety through direct human oversight.

AI can revolutionize a multitude of aspects in Martian missions, starting with mission planning and execution. By utilizing machine learning algorithms and vast datasets derived from previous missions or simulations, AI systems can predict operational challenges, identify optimal mission trajectories, and manage resource allocations with unprecedented accuracy. The complexities surrounding the interplay of various elements in a mission—like energy sustainability, scientific objectives, and system health—make AI an invaluable asset in maintaining a cohesive operational strategy.

One of the primary applications of AI in space exploration is in autonomous navigation systems. Martian rovers, which often travel across unpredictable and rugged terrain, require sophisticated navigation capabilities that can adapt to real-time conditions. Utilizing AI-driven image recognition and processing technologies, rovers can identify geological features, obstacles, and potential hazards. By employing deep learning algorithms in conjunction with Linux-based systems, these rovers can generate navigation paths dynamically, allowing them to react to unforeseen changes in their environment while significantly reducing the reliance on communication with Earth-based command centers.

The efficiency of data processing on Mars can also be enhanced through the incorporation of AI. Machine learning techniques enable systems to analyze vast volumes of scientific data generated by Martian instruments, identifying patterns and deriving insights that may be overlooked during manual analyses. For instance, AI can assist in detecting anomalies in data streams from geological sensors or atmospheric monitors, significantly accelerating the decision-making process for when to initiate specific experiments or adjust system parameters. By streamlining data interpretation, AI empowers scientists to focus their efforts on high-priority research aspects while enhancing mission outcomes.

Moreover, robotic systems designed for Martian exploration stand to benefit significantly from the integration of AI. Advancements in robotic autonomy enable tools and machines used in on-ground exploration to perform complex operational tasks without direct human instructions. By embedding AI algorithms within a Linux framework, robotic arms or rovers can learn from interactions with their environment, iteratively improving their functionality and precision over time. This capability allows robots to perform sophisticated maneuvers—for instance, analyzing soil samples, conducting repairs, or assembling structures within habitats—effectively becoming valuable collaborators in the efforts to establish a human presence on Mars.

Human-machine interactions within Martian missions also stand to gain from AI. By integrating voice recognition and natural language processing capabilities into Linux systems, the communication channels between humans and machines can be significantly enhanced. Operators can relay commands to rovers or habitat systems verbally, and the systems can respond in kind, creating a fluid dialogue. Such interactions will streamline operations, allowing mission teams to engage with technology as intuitively as they would with their team members—this is crucial in the high-stakes environment of space exploration, where time and efficiency are of the essence.

The synergy between AI and Linux is enhanced through collaborative development efforts across international space agencies and private entities. As institutions around the world contribute to the growing database of knowledge and expertise in AI, the collective impact on our missions will multiply. Open-source environments foster community-driven advancements in AI algorithms, resources, and applications, amplifying innovation across numerous projects aimed at Martian missions.

Ultimately, as we build the technological foundation that supports our endeavors on Mars and beyond, AI's role is transforming from a supplemental tool to a core component of our exploration strategies. The integration of AI within Linux systems will ensure that we are equipped with the capabilities to navigate uncertainties, analyze complex data streams, and achieve our mission objectives effectively.

In summary, the role of AI in space exploration, particularly for Mars missions, underscores its transformative potential. By leveraging AI's capabilities for autonomous navigation, data analysis, robotic systems, and facilitating human-machine interactions, we can enhance the efficiency, safety, and success of our endeavors in interplanetary exploration. As we continue this journey, the collaboration of AI and Linux will play a pivotal role in unfolding the next chapters of human exploration beyond Earth, offering unprecedented opportunities for discovery and habitation on Mars and beyond.

9.2. Autonomous Navigation Systems

In the context of Martian exploration, autonomous navigation systems represent a crucial integration of technology designed to enhance the operational capabilities of rovers, landers, and other robotic assets deployed on the planet's surface. The unpredictable terrain of Mars, coupled with the inherent communication delays between Earth and the Red Planet, underscores the critical need for systems that can navigate autonomously, make real-time decisions, and adapt to changing conditions without relying on constant oversight from mission control. To achieve this, leveraging the power of Linux as the underlying operating system provides the robustness, flexibility, and extensibility needed to execute these complex tasks effectively.

At the core of autonomous navigation systems lies the need to develop advanced perception algorithms capable of interpreting data received from an array of sensors. Rovers are typically equipped with cameras, LIDAR, ultrasonic sensors, and IMUs (Inertial Measurement Units) that provide a comprehensive view of the environment. The effective integration and interpretation of this data in real-time are paramount for obstacle detection, path planning, and movement execution. Linux-based systems can facilitate the processing of complex sensor data streams using established libraries and frameworks specifically designed for robotics, such as Robot Operating System (ROS) or OpenCV. These tools can be used to build perception models that enable rovers to identify terrains and navigate diverse landscapes, recognizing obstacles and adjusting their routes accordingly.

One significant challenge of autonomous navigation on Mars is the need for robust path planning algorithms. Given the likelihood of unexpected hazards—such as rocks, crevices, or steep inclines—rover navigation must be adaptable to ensure safety and mission success. Linux's modular architecture allows developers to implement advanced algorithms such as A, **D** Lite, or Rapidly-exploring Random Trees (RRT) for efficient pathfinding and real-time decision-making. These algorithms allow for the generation of optimal paths based on terrain analysis and environmental data while enabling on-the-fly rerouting when obstacles are encountered.

Machine learning techniques also play a vital role in refining autonomous navigation systems. By employing these algorithms, rovers can learn from previous experiences, improving their ability to navigate challenging terrains over time. Data collected during missions can be used to train models that enhance decision-making capabilities, where the system can recognize successful navigation patterns or develop predictive models for anticipated terrain challenges. By integrating machine learning into the Linux architecture of autonomous systems, rovers become increasingly capable of self-directed learning, adapting their behaviors based on empirical evidence gathered during their journeys across the Martian landscape.

Another critical component is the need for a resilient networking architecture that supports autonomous navigation. Given the communication delays and potential interruptions faced during operation, Linux systems designed for autonomous vehicles must possess the capability to function without continuous contact with mission control. This translates to the implementation of robust onboard decision-making processes and reactive protocols that empower the rover to evaluate its surroundings and adjust its behavior in real time—even in scenarios where communication is limited or temporarily severed.

Additionally, safety protocols must be woven into the design of autonomous navigation systems. Developers can program these systems with layered fail-safes, allowing the rover to engage in predefined conservative behaviors in the event of system failures, sensor anomalies or environmental disturbances. By utilizing Linux, the implementation of these mechanisms can ensure that rovers maintain operational resilience in extreme conditions.

Finally, collaboration with researchers and engineers across the globe facilitates the refinement of autonomous navigation systems. The open-source nature of Linux serves as a platform for shared knowledge and timestamped enhancements developed by a community of dedicated professionals. By collaborating on algorithms, sharing research findings, and iterating on designs, the performance of autonomous navigation systems can be continually improved.

In summary, autonomous navigation systems are integral to the success of Martian missions, powered by Linux's capabilities that align with the demands of interplanetary exploration. By utilizing advanced perception algorithms, robust path-planning techniques, machine learning, and resilient architectures, we can equip rovers with the tools necessary for effective navigation and decision-making in the unforgiving Martian environment. As we venture into this new frontier, the fusion of robotics and Linux will undoubtedly be the cornerstone of our capabilities, paving the way for exploration, discovery, and a sustained presence on Mars.

9.3. Machine Learning Applications

Machine learning stands at the forefront of transforming how we approach interplanetary exploration, particularly in the context of Mars missions where autonomous systems and advanced data processing are essential for success. By integrating machine learning algorithms into Linux-based systems, we can significantly improve mission outcomes across a variety of tasks, including navigation, data analysis, resource management, and overall operational efficiency.

At its core, machine learning allows systems to learn from data patterns and make decisions based on those insights. For Martian missions, this capability is invaluable as it empowers rovers and landers to operate autonomously in unpredictable and varied environments. By utilizing a combination of supervised and unsupervised learning techniques, machines can be trained to recognize obstacles, navigate difficult terrain, and adapt their behaviors—essential functions for ensuring safety and success on the Martian surface.

One fundamental application of machine learning in Martian missions is in the realm of autonomous navigation. Traditional methods for navigating complex terrains require pre-programmed paths, often resulting in inefficiencies as rovers encounter new challenges. By embedding machine learning algorithms within the Linux framework, we can equip these rovers with the ability to analyze their environments and make real-time, informed navigation decisions. For instance, using deep learning techniques, rovers can process imagery and sensor data to identify terrain features, such as rocks or slopes, generating optimal routes that reduce the risk of getting stuck or encountering hazards.

Data collection is another crucial area where machine learning can enhance Martian missions. Rovers and landers gather immense volumes of data from scientific instruments and environmental sensors. This information can be complex and multi-dimensional, making manual analysis impractical. Incorporating machine learning capabilities allows for the automated classification and analysis of this data, enabling systems to identify patterns linked to geological formations, atmospheric changes, or potential signs of water. By leveraging Linux's adaptability, we can create frameworks for real-time data processing that prioritize critical findings for immediate analysis or transmission back to Earth.

Moreover, machine learning can improve resource management in habitats on Mars. Systems managing water, energy, and agricultural outputs can utilize predictive analytics to ensure sustainability. For instance, if a machine learning model analyzes historical water usage data and identifies consumption patterns, it can recommend adjustments to improve efficiency and reduce waste. This adaptability and responsiveness are vital as Martian missions depend heavily on effective resource management to maintain crew health and safety.

Collaboration between rovers and other robotic systems can be streamlined through machine learning algorithms that facilitate communication and coordination. By enabling systems to learn from one another, rovers can work synergistically to complete tasks more effectively than they could independently. For instance, if one rover identifies a valuable geological feature while another is tasked with data collection, machine learning can help coordinate efforts, allowing both systems to optimize their functions and maximize research output.

In terms of operational efficiency, machine learning offers the potential for the development of predictive maintenance protocols within Linux systems. By analyzing data gathered from sensors that monitor system performance, algorithms can identify potential component failures or maintenance needs before they occur. This proactive approach helps avoid catastrophic system failures that could jeopardize missions, ultimately leading to more reliable and cost-effective operations.

The open-source nature of Linux enhances the application of machine learning in Martian missions by allowing researchers and developers to access vast libraries of algorithms and tools. This potential for collaboration fosters ongoing innovation, enabling scientists and engineers to build on one another's work and quickly adapt solutions to meet specific mission needs.

Furthermore, simulations conducted on Earth can leverage machine learning to optimize operational strategies before deployment on Mars. By modeling various scenarios, such as solar storms, dust accumulation, or resource availability, researchers can train machine learning models in controlled environments. This capability allows teams to refine algorithms and operational protocols based on empirical data before applying them in real Martian contexts.

In conclusion, the integration of machine learning into Linux-based systems for Mars missions represents a paradigm shift in how we can approach interplanetary exploration. By harnessing the power of machine learning algorithms, we empower rovers and habitats to operate autonomously, analyze complex data in real-time, manage resources efficiently, and collaborate effectively. This transformative technology not only enhances mission outcomes but also sets the foundation for sustainable human presence on Mars and beyond, fostering exploration and discovery in the cosmos. As we continue to push the boundaries of space exploration, the collaboration between Linux and machine learning will undoubtedly play a central role in shaping our future endeavors.

9.4. Robotic Systems and Linux

In the evolving landscape of robotics and space exploration, the role of Linux as an operating system tailored for the unique demands of interplanetary missions emerges as crucial, particularly when developing robotic systems designed for Mars. The intricacies of navigating and executing tasks within Martian environments necessitate the harmonious integration of cutting-edge technologies, enabling robots to operate autonomously and efficiently. The development of robust Linux-based robotics for Martian environments incorporates key aspects such as adaptability, real-time processing, and autonomous decision-making to meet the challenges of this extraterrestrial frontier.

The foundation of any successful robotic system on Mars is rooted in the design and programming of the Linux operating system to effectively harness the capabilities of onboard hardware. Engineers must prioritize lightweight, energy-efficient designs that can withstand the Martian environment—characterized by extreme temperatures, dust storms, and radiation exposure. By customizing the Linux kernel for the specific hardware architecture used in a Martian rover, developers can optimize system performance while ensuring that critical functionalities, such as data processing and sensor communication, operate seamlessly.

Robots deployed on Mars will typically be equipped with an array of sensors, cameras, and processing units. The Linux operating system enables the efficient integration of these diverse components, allowing for real-time data flow management. For instance, data collected from visual sensors can be processed concurrently with inputs from other environmental sensors, creating a comprehensive situational awareness for the robot. This capability is essential for navigating the unpredictable Martian terrain, where hazards such as rocks, crevices, and steep inclines require immediate and accurate decision-making.

An integral aspect of developing Linux-based robotic systems is enhancing their autonomy. Given the time delays in communication between Earth and Mars, robots must be capable of making independent decisions based on sensor inputs and pre-defined objectives. By leveraging artificial intelligence and machine learning algorithms—implemented within the Linux framework—robots can analyze their surroundings, recognize patterns, and adjust their behaviors accordingly. For example, a rover equipped with AI could autonomously identify geological features of interest, collect samples, and analyze data, all without waiting for instructions from mission control.

The adaptability of Linux further permits the incorporation of advanced navigation techniques, such as simultaneous localization and mapping (SLAM). This approach equips robots with the ability to construct a map of their surroundings while simultaneously tracking their position within that space. Utilizing various sensors—such as LIDAR, sonar, and cameras—Linux-based systems can execute SLAM algorithms in real-time, allowing Martian rovers to navigate complex environments with confidence and accuracy.

Additionally, the real-time processing capabilities of Linux are pivotal in robotic systems designed for Mars. Operating under varying levels of uncertainty, data must be processed rapidly to inform immediate actions. The Linux operating system supports advanced scheduling mechanisms to ensure that critical tasks—such as obstacle detection and emergency responses—are prioritized, enabling robots to react swiftly to changes in their environment. Furthermore, Linux's support for multi-threading allows for multiple operations to be conducted concurrently, further enhancing the responsiveness of robotic systems on Mars.

Another vital aspect of robotic systems is the implementation of diagnostics and monitoring features within the Linux framework. Continuous evaluations of system health, battery levels, and environmental conditions can ensure that robots remain operational over the course of their missions. By incorporating self-monitoring capabilities, Linux-based systems can detect potential malfunctions and autonomously initiate recovery procedures. For instance, if a wheel motor experiences issues, the robot may switch to an alternative route or invoke a backup system to maintain mobility, demonstrating resilience in unpredictable situations.

The inherent compatibility of Linux with other open-source software and tools fosters collaboration across international space agencies, researchers, and developers. By sharing advancements in robotic algorithms, sensor integration, and operational methodologies, the global community can collectively contribute to refining robotic systems. This fosters an environment where innovations can be rapidly iterated upon and subsequently deployed, ensuring that Martian missions benefit from the collective expertise of scientists and engineers worldwide.

Lastly, building strong human-machine interactions will play a pivotal role for robots operating in Martian terrains. Developers can leverage Linux's extensibility to create intuitive interfaces for operators on Earth, allowing them to monitor robot performance and modify objectives interactively. Human oversight, combined with machine autonomy, can establish a synergistic relationship that enhances mission outcomes—empowering operators to take advantage of their contextual knowledge while allowing robots to function independently when required.

In conclusion, the development of Linux-based robotics for Martian environments involves a multifaceted approach that integrates sensor data management, autonomous navigation, real-time processing, diagnostics, and human-machine collaboration. By harnessing the capabilities of Linux, we can equip robotic systems with the necessary tools to successfully navigate the challenges posed by Mars, advancing human exploration beyond Earth. As we move forward into this new frontier, the role of robotics powered by Linux will undoubtedly play a critical part in uncovering the mysteries of the Red Planet and laying the groundwork for humanity's continued exploration of space.

9.5. Human-Machine Interactions

In the rapidly evolving arena of space exploration, the interplay between human and machine is increasingly pivotal, particularly within the context of Martian missions. As we transition from Earth to Mars, ensuring effective human-machine interactions becomes paramount in maximizing the operational capacities of robotic systems, spacecraft, and habitats. This integration spans various fields, where engineering, psychology, and computer science converge to create systems that enhance collaboration and improve overall mission success.

Central to this endeavor is the development of intuitive interfaces that facilitate seamless communication between human operators and machines. As Linux serves as the backbone for many of the operational systems on Mars, its customizable nature allows developers to create user-friendly graphical user interfaces (GUIs) that simplify interactions. These GUIs can present complex data in digestible formats, allowing operators to monitor system performance, visualize key metrics, and issue commands with clarity and confidence. For instance, a Linux-based control panel for a rover may provide real-time telemetry alongside water and power consumption data, enabling crew members to make quick, informed decisions based on up-to-date information.

Moreover, establishing a feedback loop between human operators and machines is critical for enhancing situational awareness. Through the integration of auditory and visual alerts, operators can receive immediate notifications regarding system anomalies or required actions, ensuring that they remain informed of their machine's status at all times. By employing Linux-based systems capable of creating alerts using simple auditory cues or visual indicators, operators can prioritize their attention efficiently, allowing them to focus on critical tasks while maintaining awareness of secondary systems.

To amplify the efficiency of interactions further, leveraging artificial intelligence (AI) can unlock new capabilities for human-machine collaboration. AI algorithms can analyze sensor data and operational metrics to provide predictive insights, guiding human decision-making. For instance, if an onboard AI system detects that a rover's power levels are trending low, it can proactively suggest conservation strategies or initiate energy-saving measures automatically. By incorporating this layer of intelligence, the Linux systems onboard provide not only support but also enhance agency for human operators, allowing them to concentrate on higher-level tasks.

Furthermore, fostering a connection between robotic systems and human operators involves addressing the emotional aspect of human-machine interactions. Providing human-like responses or behaviors in robotic systems—known as social robotics—can facilitate a more intuitive and engaging relationship. By utilizing Linux to implement conversational algorithms, rovers could engage with operators through natural language processing, enabling a dialogue that fosters a sense of partnership and collaboration. This dimension is especially crucial in long-duration missions, where psychological well-being and trust in automated systems are vital components of successful human-machine interactions.

In considering the unique environmental challenges present on Mars, it becomes essential to design human-machine interfaces that account for these circumstances. The uncertainty presented by the Martian landscape, characterized by dust storms, extreme temperatures, and rugged terrain, necessitates the use of robust systems capable of functioning autonomously and with minimal direct human oversight. Meanwhile, the design must ensure operators can override automated systems when necessary, providing a check on robotic decisiveness. Linux-based systems can be programmed to balance autonomy with human control, enabling responsive systems that foster human oversight while optimizing efficiency.

Accessibility for crew members with varying levels of expertise is also an essential aspect of human-machine interactions. Linux's open-source nature allows for iterative adaptations to interfaces, ensuring that different user perspectives and needs are addressed. Creating stratified levels of interaction permits experts to dive deeply into analytical functions while offering simplified interfaces for less experienced team members. By designing Linux systems with these varied levels of interaction in mind, we can ensure effective collaboration within diverse teams.

Moreover, the training of crew members in how to interact effectively with robotic systems is paramount. Establishing an educational program that utilizes simulations and scenario-based training allows mission participants to familiarize themselves with the operational aspects of Linux-based robotic systems. Such training can include how to interpret data, react to system alerts, and engage with rovers during operations, ensuring that all personnel are equipped with the skills and knowledge needed to maximize the effectiveness of human-machine collaborations.

In conclusion, enhancing human-machine interactions within Martian missions hinges on leveraging the adaptability and flexibility of Linux-based systems to create intuitive, responsive, and intelligent interfaces. Through developing effective communication channels that prioritize situational awareness, employing predictive insights from AI, and incorporating emotional elements into robotic behaviors, we can foster a more productive collaboration between humans and machines as we explore the Red Planet. The synergy between human and machine will not only ensure mission success but can also pave the way for deeper exploration efforts, laying the groundwork for future endeavors in space exploration.

10. Building Martian Infrastructure with Linux

10.1. Developing Computational Architecture

Developing computational architecture for Martian missions involves intricate planning and design to ensure that computing systems are both robust and adaptive, capable of addressing the complexities of living and working on the Red Planet. The harsh Martian environment, characterized by extreme temperatures, radiation exposure, and dust storms, necessitates a well-thought-out approach that enhances the reliability and effectiveness of these systems. At the core of this architecture is the Linux operating system, known for its flexibility, adaptability, and open-source nature, allowing for tailored solutions suitable for the unique demands of space exploration.

The foundation of a robust computational architecture must begin with an understanding of the hardware on which the systems will run. Given the limited resources available for missions to Mars, selecting lightweight, energy-efficient computing hardware is paramount. This involves utilizing high-performance components that can withstand radiation and operate under extreme environmental conditions. The architecture should incorporate radiation-hardened processors, durable memory systems, and energy-efficient power supplies. By leveraging the capabilities of Linux, systems can be designed to monitor hardware status in real-time, tracking the health of critical components and enabling predictive maintenance protocols.

A crucial aspect of the computational architecture involves the establishment of versatile server systems. These servers act as the backbone for data processing, storage, and distribution, facilitating communication between various mission components—rovers, habitats, and scientific instruments. The Linux operating system excels in handling server functionalities, supporting multiple users, processes, and network protocols simultaneously. Configuring a centralized data management system using Linux allows for efficient data flow, ensuring that information collected from Martian environments is processed and transmitted back to Earth adequately.

Distributed computing models also play a significant role in the computational architecture designed for Mars. This decentralized approach allows for collaboration among various systems across the Mars network, where computation and processing resources are shared seamlessly. Additionally, using distributed systems minimizes the reliance on single points of failure—crucial when operating in a remote environment where system failures may lead to mission-threatening situations. By implementing Linux, the architecture can support containerization technologies that enable each component —be it a rover or a habitat monitoring system—to operate independently while still being part of a coordinated framework.

An essential feature of the computational architecture is the implementation of redundancy and failover mechanisms. Given the unpredictability of the Martian environment, ensuring continued operation in the face of hardware or software failures is critical. The architecture should facilitate automated failover protocols—where backup systems take over functions if the primary systems fail—ensuring mission objectives can continue without interruption. Using Linux, developers can create highly resilient operational frameworks where regular health checks on both hardware and software are initiated, enabling quick response actions to any anomalies detected.

Moreover, cybersecurity remains an integral concern when developing computational architecture for Mars. As systems become interconnected, they become vulnerable to potential threats, whether from environmental effects or intentional tampering. Employing advanced security measures is crucial in safeguarding communication lines and maintaining the integrity of data. Practices such as encryption protocols, secure communication channels, and strict access control mechanisms can be integrated within the Linux framework to ensure that all transmitted information remains protected against unauthorized access. Regular updates and patches, facilitated by the open-source community, will help to address vulnerabilities and bolster overall system security.

Furthermore, the design of the computational architecture should allow for future expansion and adaptation, anticipating the emergence of new technologies and challenges that may arise during Martian missions. As exploration advances, updating the systems to accommodate innovations—such as developments in artificial intelligence for data processing or energy management—will be vital to sustainability and scientific progress. Linux's customizable nature ensures that legacy systems can be enhanced with new tools, frameworks, and applications without the need for complete system overhauls.

In summary, developing computational architecture for Martian missions involves a multifaceted approach that leverages the flexibility of Linux to create robust, reliable, and adaptive systems. By focusing on the integration of durable hardware, establishing versatile server systems, utilizing distributed computing models, implementing redundancy protocols, enhancing cybersecurity measures, and ensuring adaptability for future technological advancements, we can set the stage for successful exploration and habitation on Mars. This foundation will ultimately empower humanity to push the boundaries of our interplanetary endeavors, transforming the vision of Mars as a second home into a tangible reality.

10.2. Robust Server Systems

Robust server systems are a cornerstone of mission infrastructure as we prepare for exploration on Mars and beyond. These systems are pivotal in managing the myriad data-driven tasks that will arise during our endeavors on the Red Planet, encompassing everything from communications with Earth, navigation for rovers, environmental monitoring, and life support systems for human habitats. Building such robust server systems involves multiple considerations critical to their successful deployment and operation in the Martian environment.

At the forefront of establishing reliable server systems is the selection of appropriate hardware. Given Mars' unique challenges—including extreme temperatures, intermittent dust storms, and cosmic radiation—servers must be engineered using rugged components that can withstand these harsh conditions. This means choosing radiation-hardened CPUs and memory modules that offer enhanced reliability and signal integrity. Utilizing Linux as the operating system enhances this endeavor, as it supports a broad range of hardware architectures while providing options for tailored configurations suitable for specific tasks.

Once hardware is settled, attention turns to how the server systems will be structured and deployed. The architecture must emphasize modularity and scalability to accommodate evolving mission requirements. For example, missions may need to expand their capabilities by deploying additional sensors or communication devices, necessitating a system that can seamlessly scale up without requiring a complete overhaul. Through Linux's support for containerization technologies, such as Docker, mission planners can develop modular server environments that allow for the easy addition or removal of functional components as needed. This level of flexibility is paramount, enabling quick adaptations to changing mission parameters or goals.

Moreover, robust server systems must incorporate redundancy and failover mechanisms to mitigate the risks stemming from potential hardware failures. Given the considerable distance between Mars and Earth, support for direct intervention is limited; thus, maintaining operational continuity becomes critical. With Linux, developers can design server architectures that implement automatic failover protocols—where backup systems assume control should primary systems fail. This greatly enhances reliability, ensuring that mission-critical services remain available even in the face of unexpected challenges.

Effective data management is another key consideration in developing robust server systems. Rovers and habitats will generate vast amounts of data that require secure storage and efficient processing. The Linux operating system supports various file systems optimized for high performance and reliability, enabling substantial datasets to be effectively organized, stored, and retrieved. Implementing distributed computing models that allow data to be processed in parallel across multiple servers can further enhance performance, particularly during busy operational periods when data influxes accelerate.

Linux-based server systems must also employ cyber security measures to safeguard mission data and communications. Operating in a remote environment increases vulnerability to potential external threats, be it from unintentional interference or malicious entities. Security measures such as encrypted communications, strict access controls, and regular security audits of server systems need to be integrated seamlessly within the Linux environment. By adopting best practices derived from the open-source community, Linux offers a wealth of resources to implement up-to-date security protocols that help protect against breaches.

Lastly, maintaining continuous communication with Earth requires that robust server systems support effective data transmission protocols. As Mars missions will face challenges related to latency and bandwidth, servers must be equipped not only to handle large data loads during peak periods but also to efficiently process important updates when bandwidth is constrained. This involves designing systems that can package data effectively for transmission and prioritize critical information to ensure timely communication without overload.

In conclusion, developing robust server systems for Martian missions entails a comprehensive approach that combines careful hardware selection, modular architecture, redundancy strategies, efficient data management, cybersecurity measures, and efficient communication protocols. Utilizing Linux as the operating system provides an exceptional foundation for these systems, offering the adaptability and robustness needed to support our explorative efforts on Mars and beyond. As we continue this journey, the emphasis on building resilient server systems will be pivotal in actualizing our vision for interplanetary exploration, enabling humanity to thrive in new and distant realms.

10.3. Distributed Computing Models

Distributed computing models are vital for enhancing the capabilities of Martian networks, facilitating seamless collaboration between various robotic systems, habitats, and mission control on Earth. As we embark on this ambitious journey of interplanetary exploration, the effective integration of distributed computing architectures within a Linux framework becomes indispensable in addressing the challenges posed by communication delays, resource management, and environmental unpredictability on Mars.

At the heart of distributed computing is the ability to decentralize processes, allowing multiple systems to work in parallel rather than relying solely on a centralized server. This capability is particularly advantageous in the context of Martian exploration, where data must be collected, processed, and shared among a variety of components deployed across the planet. For instance, rovers equipped with sensors can gather geological or atmospheric data autonomously while communicating their findings to a central Linux server or cloud storage system, which may reside either on Mars or back on Earth. This model not only enhances data acquisition speed but also enables real-time analysis of data feeds, resulting in quicker decision-making and operational adjustments.

Linux's open-source architecture is well-suited for implementing distributed computing models. It supports a multitude of programming frameworks and tools that facilitate the development of distributed applications, such as Apache Hadoop or Kubernetes. Engineers can build a network of Linux-based nodes acting as independent processing units, each with a specific function—whether collecting data, managing power consumption, or ensuring system stability. By harnessing the flexibility of Linux, mission planners can tailor these systems to meet the unique requirements of their Martian objectives while enabling scalability for future missions.

Moreover, effective distributed computing models must consider the inherent communication delays between Earth and Mars, which can range from several minutes to over twenty-four minutes. To ensure smooth operations under these constraints, it is essential to implement local decision-making capabilities within each distributed node. By equipping rovers and habitats with Linux-based systems capable of analyzing data and making autonomous decisions, mission success can be ensured even when communication with Earth is delayed or interrupted. This ability to operate independently is crucial for maintaining autonomy and efficiency in Martian environments, where human oversight is often limited.

Another key component of distributed computing models is the establishment of reliable data-sharing protocols among interconnected systems. In a Martian context, with multiple rovers, landers, and habitats all potentially collecting diverse datasets, ensuring that this information is transmitted securely and efficiently is paramount. By utilizing Linux's robust networking capabilities, mission planners can establish secure protocols that facilitate the dissemination of data across various nodes without compromising the integrity or confidentiality of the information collected. This seamless data flow fosters collaboration, enabling the entire mission ecosystem to respond more effectively to unexpected challenges.

Additionally, leveraging machine learning algorithms within distributed computing models can enhance the efficiency of data processing and improve overall system performance. By utilizing Linux's support for advanced data analytics frameworks, rovers can be equipped with machine learning algorithms that allow them to learn from previous missions and optimize their behaviors in real-time. This capability enables automated systems to make data-driven decisions and improve their operational processes, ultimately leading to more effective missions and resource utilization.

As we venture into the depths of space, scalability must also be at the forefront of our distributed computing models. Future missions to Mars and beyond may involve a greater number of robotic systems or the establishment of permanent bases. By designing a flexible distributed architecture within the Linux framework, mission planners can ensure that new systems can be integrated smoothly into existing networks, supporting a wide array of functions and continuing to enhance the overall mission infrastructure.

Finally, collaboration among international partners can be greatly amplified through distributed computing models. Several space agencies and organizations may contribute their technologies, data, and expertise in designing Martian missions. By adopting a shared Linux environment, these partnerships can streamline integration processes, fostering efficient cooperation that enhances the capabilities and outcomes of interplanetary exploration.

In conclusion, distributed computing models represent a transformative approach to enhancing Martian networks, allowing for seamless collaboration, real-time decision-making, and effective data processing. By leveraging the flexibility, scalability, and adaptability of Linux, mission planners can create robust and resilient systems capable of navigating the complexities of interplanetary exploration. As we continue our journey to Mars and beyond, these models will serve as a cornerstone of our technological infrastructure, empowering humanity to explore the cosmos with confidence and effectiveness.

10.4. Redundancy and Failover Mechanisms

In the realm of space exploration, redundancy and failover mechanisms are critical to ensure the reliability and continuity of systems deployed in the harsh environments of planets like Mars. The nature of interplanetary missions is inherently uncertain; varying environmental conditions, the challenges of remote operation, and the risks of hardware failure necessitate robust strategies to maintain system integrity and functionality. As we prepare for Martian exploration with Linux as our operating system of choice, understanding how redundancy and failover systems can be effectively implemented will be essential to achieving our mission objectives.

Redundancy refers to the incorporation of backup components or systems designed to take over in the event of a primary system failure. This principle is especially vital in space exploration, where communication with Earth may be delayed or nonexistent following an equipment failure. By implementing redundancy at various levels —be it in hardware, software, or network resources—mission planners can significantly increase the resilience of systems operating on Mars. For example, deploying multiple sensors to monitor ambient environmental conditions allows the system to continue functioning if one sensor fails, ensuring continuous data acquisition and situational awareness.

Failover mechanisms work hand in hand with redundancy, acting as the protocols that automatically switch control from a failing component to its backup. In the context of a Linux-based system operating on Mars, these mechanisms can be encapsulated in software routines that monitor the health status of critical systems in real-time. Should an anomaly be detected in a primary sensor or processing unit—such as a temperature sensor exceeding defined thresholds or a processing node exhibiting unusual behavior—the failover protocol would activate the secondary system, minimizing system downtime and maintaining operational capabilities seamlessly.

One practical example of redundancy and failover in Linux-based systems deployed on Mars includes applying dual-redundant power supplies for critical hardware. Should one power supply fail, the backup immediately engages to provide uninterrupted power, ensuring that essential systems remain operational. Implementing such redundancy helps protect against power management failures that could disrupt crucial activities such as scientific analysis or life support operations.

In addition to hardware redundancy, software systems must also be designed with failover capabilities. Linux's modular architecture allows for multiple instances of applications to be running simultaneously. If one instance becomes unresponsive or crashes, a parallel instance can immediately take over. By creating health monitoring checks that regularly assess system and application statuses, Linux can automatically reroute processes to operational counterparts, ensuring that mission-critical functionalities remain intact.

Network redundancy is another aspect worth exploring. With communication channels being a vital link to mission control on Earth, designing networks that incorporate multiple pathways for data transmission significantly enhances resilience. Linux provides network management capabilities that can seamlessly switch between different communication routes, whether through terrestrial links, satellite relays, or even localized mesh networks among multiple Martian vehicles, reinforcing the overall integrity of communications.

An integral component of developing redundancy and failover mechanisms is the aspect of thorough testing and verification. Before launching any systems to Mars, engineers must conduct rigorous simulations that replicate potential failure scenarios. By stress-testing the entire system—including failover protocols and backup operations—developers can identify weaknesses and refine the strategies necessary to mitigate risks. Utilizing Linux in these testing phases allows for rapid iteration, as modifications can be implemented dynamically based on simulations. This iterative process supports the establishment of reliable systems capable of enduring the challenges posed by the Martian environment.

Additionally, the human factor must be considered in redundancy and failover mechanisms. Occupants on Mars—whether astronauts or robotic operators—should be trained on the operational protocols pertinent to these systems. Familiarity with the failover processes enables crew members to understand the mechanics of system failures and confidently intervene when necessary. Creating training programs that incorporate scenario-based learning using simulations powered by Linux can enhance crew preparedness for any eventuality.

With the ever-evolving landscape of space exploration needs and challenges, conducting regular updates of Linux systems carrying redundancy and failover features is equally essential. By tapping into the community-driven nature of open-source software, ongoing improvements and enhancements can lead to even more robust systems. Maintaining regular dialogue with industries and scholars specializing in reliability engineering and space systems can further enrich the contemporary understanding of redundancy requirements.

In conclusion, the implementation of redundancy and failover mechanisms in Linux-based systems is paramount for ensuring the reliability and continuity of operations on Martian missions. By focusing on hardware, software, and network redundancies, we can significantly enhance resilience against failures, allowing systems to endure the unpredictability of the Martian environment. With careful design, rigorous testing, and community-driven improvement, we pave the way for successful missions, ensuring that as we venture into space, we are well-prepared for the unexpected. Ultimately, our commitment to redundancy will be a cornerstone of achieving our ambitious objectives for exploration and habitation on Mars and beyond.

10.5. Cybersecurity Challenges and Solutions

In the contemporary landscape of space exploration, the importance of cybersecurity has never been more pronounced, especially as we prepare for complex missions to Mars and potentially beyond. The unique challenges posed by operating in an extraterrestrial environment, combined with the intricacies of communicating across vast distances, render cybersecurity an essential component of mission planning and execution. As we deploy Linux systems to manage various operations on Mars—from landers and rovers to habitats and communications networks—it is vital that we address the myriad cybersecurity threats that could jeopardize mission integrity and safety.

A critical challenge lies in the sheer volume of data being generated, transmitted, and processed during Martian missions. As rovers traverse the landscape, collecting invaluable scientific data, the risk of interception or corruption of this information during transmission must be considered. The distance between Earth and Mars introduces latency issues, but it also presents opportunities for malicious actors to exploit weaknesses in communication pathways. Therefore, employing encryption protocols is paramount; using Linux's capabilities, we can ensure that all data transmitted between Martian systems and mission control on Earth is securely encrypted, preventing unauthorized access and safeguarding sensitive scientific findings.

Moreover, the variety of interconnected systems operating on Mars introduces numerous potential points of vulnerability. Each device or application running on Linux must adhere to strict access control policies to mitigate the risk of infiltration. Implementing role-based access controls (RBAC) ensures that only authorized personnel have the ability to interact with mission-critical systems, reducing the likelihood of accidental or malicious disruptions. Given the collaborative nature of space missions, where teams from different organizations may work together, it is imperative that strict protocols are in place to control access while maintaining the necessary flexibility to allow for effective collaboration.

In addition to traditional cybersecurity measures, robust monitoring systems must be established to identify and respond to anomalies in real-time. Linux's logging capabilities can be leveraged to create comprehensive records of system performance and user activities. By integrating intrusion detection and prevention systems (IDPS), we can actively monitor for unusual patterns or behaviors that could indicate a potential security breach. These systems can automatically trigger responses, such as alerting mission control or enacting predefined containment protocols. This proactive approach fosters a culture of vigilance and responsiveness, ensuring that cybersecurity remains a priority throughout the duration of missions.

The physical environment of Mars itself poses unique challenges to cybersecurity. With potential exposure to extreme cosmic radiation, systems must be designed to withstand electronic disruptions. Implementing radiation-hardened components within the Linux architecture is critical. In conjunction with robust software protocols, these elements together build resilience against radiation-induced errors that could compromise system integrity. Linux allows for the implementation of error-checking routines and redundancy protocols to recover from failure, enhancing operational reliability.

Another significant consideration is the potential for adversarial interventions or cyberattacks targeting systems that govern operations on Mars. The militarization of space is an emerging issue, and as we deploy technology on other celestial bodies, we must remain vigilant against potential geopolitical conflicts manifesting in cyberspace. To solidify our defense against such threats, we need to foster international standards for cybersecurity in space exploration. Collaboration with global partners to establish best practices and sharing knowledge on protecting mission-critical systems will enhance the collective resilience of all robotic systems operating off-world.

Moreover, as artificial intelligence and machine learning become integrated components of Martian operational systems, ethical cybersecurity considerations are paramount. The automation of decision-making protocols can introduce vulnerabilities, and it is essential that comprehensive guidelines are established governing how AI systems operate in the context of cybersecurity. By embedding transparency measures in the design of AI algorithms, we can ensure that operators have oversight over decision-making processes and that accountability mechanisms are in place to address any potential security failures.

Finally, NASA and other space agencies must remain committed to ongoing education and training concerning cybersecurity protocols. As new technologies evolve, it is crucial that personnel are continually updated on the latest threats and defenses. This training should include situational awareness on recognizing potential vulnerabilities and the importance of establishing a strong cybersecurity culture throughout mission operations.

In conclusion, addressing cybersecurity challenges in Martian missions requires a comprehensive, proactive approach that integrates robust strategies within the Linux environment. By leveraging encryption protocols, implementing strict access controls, establishing continuous monitoring, investing in hardware resilience, nurturing international cooperation, and educating personnel, we can build a robust cybersecurity framework that safeguards the integrity and success of our exploratory missions. As we step into the new frontier of Mars and beyond, ensuring the security of our systems will be instrumental in realizing the full potential of human exploration in outer space.

11. Beyond Mars: Linux and the Broader Solar System

11.1. Solar System Exploration Opportunities

As humanity looks to the stars and sets its sights on Mars as a potential new home, the exploration of our solar system beyond this red planet offers vast opportunities for scientific discovery, technological innovation, and human expansion. The unique challenges of operating in extraterrestrial environments require careful planning and robust technology capable of adapting to the demands of space. Linux, with its open-source philosophy, flexibility, and community-driven development, stands as a pivotal component in these ambitious explorations.

One of the primary opportunities for solar system exploration lies in the rich array of celestial bodies within our reach, each presenting unique environments and scientific questions. For instance, moons such as Europa and Enceladus contain subsurfaces of water that may harbor conditions suitable for life, attracting interest from astrobiologists and planetary scientists alike. These icy bodies offer the promise of revealing the mechanisms that support life, and embarking on missions to study them could yield groundbreaking insights. Linux systems can be integral to managing the autonomous vehicles and landers needed to navigate these challenging icy terrains, equipped with advanced sensors and capable of performing real-time data analysis to capture vital information.

The potential for exploring asteroids is another exciting avenue. The asteroid belt, rich in resources, offers prospects for mining and the possibility of retrieving materials for future human settlements or technological applications. Missions designed to study asteroids can utilize Linux to develop sophisticated navigation and sensor systems, enabling spacecraft to approach and analyze these small bodies' orbits and compositions autonomously. Combining robotic spacecraft with mining technologies could pave the way for sustainable resource harvesting, providing materials for use in both space and on Earth.

The dynamic nature of our solar system fosters opportunities for cross-planetary missions, well-coordinated through the adaptability of Linux in managing mission logistics, communication, and science operations. With the detox of its capabilities, Linux provides the framework needed to develop interplanetary vehicles capable of navigating the varying conditions all planets and moons present. It can manage vital systems for propulsion, energy generation, and communications—allowing for cross-planetary exploratory missions that enhance our understanding of the solar system and how planetary bodies interact within it.

As we engineer missions that embrace the diversity of our solar system, compatibility with emerging technologies becomes necessary. Technologies such as advanced propulsion systems (e.g., ion propulsion, solar sails), autonomous drones, and advanced robotics are vital for navigating and operating in low-gravity environments. Ensuring that Linux remains compatible with these technologies will be essential for maximizing operational efficiency and addressing the challenges they present. By establishing an adaptable software architecture that accommodates innovations in hardware and software, mission planners can leverage advancements in propulsion or sensors to enhance mission capabilities while maintaining a sustainable development strategy.

International collaboration is also key as we embark on multi-planetary missions. Engaging global partners in the design and execution of shared missions fosters a unified approach to exploring our solar system while pooling resources, expertise, and technological capabilities. By adopting Linux as a standardized operating system framework for across international space agencies, we can streamline collaboration and ensure that systems developed for various missions can work seamlessly together. This cooperation can extend to sharing scientific data collected from various celestial bodies, promoting transparency and accelerating discoveries.

Finally, as we look to the future, the visionary potential of Linux in space exploration cannot be overstated. The ongoing evolution of technology will inevitably present new challenges as humanity explores deeper into the cosmos. Whether it entails innovations driven by artificial intelligence, advancements in material science, or cutting-edge communication systems, Linux's adaptability will be key in sustaining explorative pursuits. By fostering a culture of continuous development and open-source collaboration, Linux can lead the charge in shaping the frameworks that govern exploration, ensuring we are well-prepared for whatever awaits us in the vast expanse of space.

In summary, the exploration of our solar system beyond Mars is replete with opportunities that hold the promise of unlocking new secrets about our universe, forging paths toward human settlement, and expanding scientific knowledge has never been more tangible. By leveraging the strengths of Linux, we can pivot toward a future where meaningful exploration can lead to sustainable advancements, enhancing humanity's understanding of the cosmic landscape that exists beyond our planet. As we venture forth, Linux stands ready to support us in harnessing these opportunities for the benefit of all humankind.

11.2. Cross-Planetary Mission Planning

Cross-Planetary Mission Planning is a pivotal aspect of contemporary space exploration, particularly as we set our sights not only on Mars but also on the exploration of other celestial bodies within our solar system. The complexity of multi-planetary missions requires meticulous planning, system integrations, collaborative efforts among international partners, and the employment of advanced technologies. In this section, we will explore the critical components that underpin the successful planning of cross-planetary missions, emphasizing how Linux can serve as the backbone for these ambitious endeavors.

At the forefront of cross-planetary mission planning is the need for robust mission architecture that encompasses the objectives, timelines, logistics, and resource management strategies required to ensure successful operations. This architecture must be designed to accommodate the unique challenges presented by each destination, whether it be the moon, an asteroid, or the icy bodies of Europa and Enceladus. Key to this planning process is the establishment of clear goals that drive the development of technical systems, define operational protocols, and inform the overall mission strategy.

The utilization of Linux as the operating system for mission-critical systems becomes central to efficiently managing diverse technologies involved in cross-planetary communications and operations. The inherent flexibility and adaptability of Linux allow it to be customized to meet the specific operational requirements of different spacecraft, rovers, and habitat systems. Through an open-source architecture, mission planners can leverage community-driven development efforts, ensuring that the latest advancements in software and algorithms are integrated seamlessly into their mission framework.

One significant aspect of planning multi-planetary missions involves effectively managing interplanetary communication. Given the vast distances between planets, communication delays inherent to interplanetary travel present unique challenges. Travelers to destinations such as Mars or beyond will experience latency ranging from minutes to hours for signal transmission. Advanced algorithms running on Linux systems can be established to prioritize data transmission based on urgency, ensuring that mission-critical communications are sent promptly. For instance, in the event of a scientific discovery, data from rovers or landers can be prioritized for transmission, maximizing the value of each communication session with mission control.

Another critical component is navigation planning, which involves developing protocols for guiding robotic systems and crewed missions through complex environments. Utilizing real-time data processing capabilities offered by Linux, mission planners can implement autonomous navigation algorithms that allow rovers to assess their surroundings, identify hazards, and adapt their paths dynamically. These algorithms must be rigorously tested and continually refined to account for the multitude of variables present during space operations, including irregular terrain, dust storms, and changing atmospheric conditions.

Resource management also plays a crucial role in cross-planetary mission planning, particularly with an emphasis on sustainability. Developing strategies for efficiently utilizing limited supplies, such as energy, water, and food, is of paramount importance. Linux systems can support the deployment of integrated resource management frameworks that monitor consumption, identify inefficiencies, and optimize resource allocation throughout the mission. Ensuring that habitats maintain self-sustainability while minimizing reliance on Earth resupply becomes an essential aspect of mission planning for the long-term ambitions of cross-planetary exploration.

International collaboration is another fundamental pillar of successful cross-planetary mission planning. Engaging global partners enhances the exchange of technological innovations, scientific knowledge, and operational best practices. By adopting Linux as a common operating platform, space agencies around the world can streamline the integration of various systems, allowing different robotic missions and spacecraft to communicate seamlessly. This collaborative framework could potentially unify efforts in technology development for planetary missions, leading to shared discoveries and accelerating our understanding of the solar system.

As plans for cross-planetary missions emerge, it is crucial to embrace adaptability and ensure that contingencies are woven into the fabric of mission plans. The dynamic nature of space exploration means that unforeseen challenges will inevitably arise. By prioritizing iterative development and ongoing assessment of mission objectives, mission planners can adjust strategies as conditions change—ensuring that missions remain on track despite potential obstacles that may surface during operational phases.

In conclusion, cross-planetary mission planning requires a multifaceted approach that integrates robust mission architecture, effective communication strategies, autonomous navigation, resource management, international collaboration, and adaptability to dynamic conditions. By leveraging the capabilities of Linux as an operating system that can support diverse technologies and promote collaboration among international partners, we can significantly enhance our ability to explore our solar system beyond Mars. As humanity ventures into this new frontier, careful planning and execution will pave the way for unprecedented opportunities in space exploration, knowledge acquisition, and ultimately, the ongoing quest for life beyond Earth.

11.3. Compatibility with Emerging Technologies

In the context of space exploration, especially as we prepare for missions to Mars and beyond, the compatibility of operating systems like Linux with emerging technologies is pivotal in shaping the trajectory of our interstellar endeavors. The rapid advancements in technology, coupled with the unique challenges posed by extraterrestrial environments, necessitate an adaptive approach that can integrate various innovations seamlessly. Understanding how Linux can be aligned with new technological developments not only enhances mission effectiveness but also provides a versatile framework that accommodates future requirements.

One of the foremost areas in which compatibility plays a critical role is in the integration of artificial intelligence (AI) and machine learning (ML) within Linux-driven systems. As robotic systems deployed on Mars increasingly leverage AI algorithms for autonomous navigation and decision-making, ensuring that these technologies are compatible with Linux architectures is essential. For instance, the ability to run advanced neural networks for image recognition or terrain analysis on Linux allows rovers to interpret their environments more effectively and adapt their actions in real-time. The open-source nature of Linux enables developers to access a wealth of tools and libraries, fostering an ecosystem that promotes the continuous evolution of AI applications tailored for space exploration.

Furthermore, as space agencies shift their focus to resource utilization technologies, such as in-situ resource utilization (ISRU) for water and oxygen generation, Linux systems must be equipped to incorporate these innovations seamlessly. Ensuring compatibility with emerging hardware and software protocols related to resource management directly impacts the sustainability of life support systems aboard habitats. By leveraging Linux's modular architecture, developers can create applications that interface with ISRU technologies—such as chemical processors or solar-powered water extraction systems— ensuring efficient operation and resource optimization.

The advent of advanced communication technologies, including satellite networks and laser-based communication systems, further emphasizes the need for Linux compatibility. As we envision networked architectures that facilitate real-time data transmission between multiple rovers or habitats and mission control on Earth, Linux must remain at the forefront of technological adaptability. The ability to integrate new communication protocols into existing Linux frameworks will facilitate improved data transfer rates and allow for redundancy strategies that maintain connectivity during adverse Martian weather conditions, such as dust storms.

Moreover, the compatibility of Linux with advancements in robotics and automation technology is paramount for creating resilient exploratory systems. As robotic capabilities evolve, incorporating machine learning-driven automatic control systems into Linux allows for enhanced operational functionalities. For example, rovers will become increasingly adept at performing complex tasks, from sample collection to geological analysis, all while operating independently with minimal human oversight. This future-oriented approach emphasizes the necessity for Linux to continuously adapt to new robotics technologies and support their development.

Collaboration with international partners also underscores the importance of Linux compatibility with emerging technologies. In the spirit of open-source development, the adaptability of Linux fosters fruitful collaborations among space agencies and research institutions globally. As various organizations contribute to enhancing software capabilities for interplanetary missions, a unified approach built around Linux allows for the seamless exchange of innovations. When different teams can work together on shared platforms, they can optimize systems for specific environments, exchanging knowledge related to cutting-edge technologies, methodologies, and best practices.

Furthermore, the potential emergence of distributed computing models and quantum computing capabilities presents new horizons for Linux compatibility. As we explore the capabilities of applying these advanced technologies to Mars missions, it is crucial that Linux systems can support hybrid environments that blend traditional architectures with next-generation innovations. The flexibility of Linux ensures that as technological paradigms shift, mission planners can adapt swiftly without significant disruption to ongoing operations.

In refining Linux for compatibility with various emerging technologies, a robust strategy involving thorough testing and simulation becomes essential. Developers must engage in high-fidelity simulations on Earth that closely mimic the unique challenges of Martian environments. This iterative process will allow them to evaluate the compatibility of new technologies with existing systems, make essential adjustments, and optimize performance ahead of deployment.

In conclusion, the compatibility of Linux with emerging technologies is foundational to advancing our missions in space exploration, especially as we turn our attention toward Mars and other celestial bodies. By harnessing Linux's adaptability, we can optimize the integration of AI, improve resource utilization frameworks, advance communication systems, and enhance robotics capabilities—all critical elements for ensuring the success of interplanetary endeavors. As we forge ahead in this new era of exploration, prioritizing compatibility will empower us to leverage the full potential of innovative technologies and redefine our aspirations for the future of humanity beyond Earth.

11.4. Co-Development with International Partners

In the ever-evolving landscape of space exploration, co-development with international partners represents a harmonious blend of expertise, innovation, and shared ambition. As we aim toward ambitious missions to Mars and beyond, the complexities of space exploration necessitate the collaboration of a wide array of entities, including space agencies, private companies, academic institutions, and research organizations. Leveraging the strengths of open-source technologies, particularly Linux, serves as a catalyst for successfully navigating the challenges of interplanetary missions through collaborative efforts.

Collaboration in space exploration is not merely a matter of pooling resources; it represents the intersection of diverse perspectives and expertise from around the globe. Each international partner brings unique insights and capabilities, fostering an enriching environment ripe for innovation. For example, by uniting various countries' engineering, scientific, and technological strengths, the co-development of systems for Mars missions minimizes redundancy while enhancing the overall capabilities of the mission. Such collaboration has precedent in endeavors like the International Space Station (ISS), a pinnacle of shared international efforts in space, where shared technologies and cooperative research have laid the groundwork for future missions.

At the heart of this cooperative effort is the open-source ethos that governs Linux, an operating system ideally suited for interconnected systems and projects. The collaborative nature of Linux enables developers and engineers from different countries to work together in real time, sharing code, ideas, and advancements without the constraints that often accompany proprietary systems. With multiple teams improving or modifying the same Linux-based technologies, the resultant diversity accelerates the pace of innovation, allowing for a more rapid response to challenges within space exploration missions.

One of the most significant aspects of co-development is the establishment of standardized processes and protocols. As various countries contribute to the development of technology and systems for Martian missions, ensuring that all components are produced and operate on compatible standards is essential. By leveraging Linux as the common operating platform, collaborators can more easily integrate different applications, hardware, and protocols, allowing teams from different nations to contribute their respective technologies to the collective mission effectively. This standardization not only fosters interoperability but also streamlines the integration process, ultimately ensuring a cohesive operational system on Mars.

Another cornerstone of co-development lies in the engagement of data sharing and collaborative research initiatives. As different partners contribute their findings and insights from ongoing experiments, the collective knowledge enhances the efficacy of mission planning and execution. For instance, data collected from previous missions such as the Mars Exploration Rovers provides valuable information that can guide the design and operational protocols for new robotic systems. By fostering a culture of open data sharing among international partners, insights gained can benefit all projects, amplifying the value derived from scientific endeavors.

Furthermore, the co-development of infrastructure and logistics for space missions necessitates the coordination of launch vehicles, spacecraft, and robotic systems in conjunction with international partners. This requires a focus on developing logistical frameworks that consider the capabilities of each partner's technology and resources while ensuring a streamlined approach to mission execution. By working together to share expertise in launch planning, mission management, and operational safety, international partners can create a resilient architecture that enhances mission viability.

The aspect of training also becomes a critical consideration in co-development initiatives, ensuring that personnel involved in missions across partner agencies are proficient in utilizing shared technologies. By designing joint training programs that utilize Linux-based systems, collaborators can familiarize team members with the operational interfaces and specific tools employed during missions. This not only strengthens the competence of mission personnel but also fosters collaboration, enabling a deeper understanding of each partner's capabilities and methodologies.

While the emphasis here is on collaboration, it is equally important to consider the ethical implications of sharing technology and knowledge among nations. Establishing clear agreements and governance structures regarding intellectual property rights, technology transfers, and shared resources will pave the way for mutually beneficial partnerships. These considerations are especially critical in ensuring that advancements derived from collaborative projects contribute to the broader goals of humanity and pave the way for our future in space exploration.

In summary, co-development with international partners is fundamental to successfully advancing our missions to Mars and beyond. By leveraging the strengths of Linux as an open-source platform, we can foster a collaborative environment that enhances innovation, productivity, and mutual benefit. The union of diverse expertise and perspectives positions us to confront the immense challenges of space exploration while enhancing our ability to unlock the secrets of the cosmos. As we forge partnerships in the name of exploration, the spirit of cooperation will be our guiding star in the quest for knowledge and understanding on our celestial neighbors.

11.5. The Visionary Future of Linux in Space

In the era of space exploration, the critical role that Linux is poised to play in shaping the future of interplanetary missions cannot be overstated. As we stand on the brink of sending humans to Mars and beyond, the versatility, adaptability, and collaborative ethos of Linux positions it to become an indispensable tool for the challenges that lie ahead. The future of Linux in space represents not only the advancement of technology but also a transformative vision that bridges humanity's ambitions with the vast possibilities of the cosmos.

To begin with, the continued evolution of Linux as a flexible and open-source operating system allows for rapid innovation in response to the ever-changing landscape of space exploration. The open-source community acts as a powerful engine for developing new software, tools, and applications, all tailored to fit the unique demands of extraterrestrial environments. By fostering a culture of collaboration among international space agencies, academic institutions, and private enterprises, Linux will serve as a common framework upon which technological advancements can flourish—allowing for the quick adaptation and integration of emerging technologies into existing systems.

In the upcoming exploratory missions to Mars, Linux is expected to play a pivotal role in managing autonomous systems and robotics. As the complexities of Martian navigation and data acquisition escalate, the reliance on intelligent, autonomous robotic systems will increase. These systems, powered by advanced AI algorithms running on Linux, will need to operate independently, making real-time decisions about navigation, scientific analysis, and resource usage. The vision of autonomous rovers, landers, and drones carrying out exploratory missions seamlessly, adapting to environmental changes, and collaborating on scientific objectives is not just aspirational; it is plausible, driven by the capabilities of Linux.

Moreover, as we extend our gaze beyond Mars to the outer planets and their moons, including destinations like Europa and Titan, Linux will be instrumental in creating a cohesive technological ecosystem. The potential for long-term human or robotic presence on these distant bodies will necessitate robust habitats equipped with life support systems, resource utilization technologies, and powerful communication networks. Linux's agility will facilitate the integration of these systems, allowing mission planners to optimize habitat design, develop sophisticated environmental controls, and establish responsive data management protocols that support sustainable living in extreme conditions.

In addition to technical advancements, the future of Linux in space embodies a paradigm shift towards democratization and inclusivity in space exploration. The open-source nature of Linux allows for widespread participation from developers, engineers, and enthusiasts around the world. This inclusive approach encourages global collaboration, enabling diverse perspectives to contribute to the design and execution of interplanetary missions. As we leverage the collective knowledge and experience of the global community, we can foster equity in access to space exploration, expanding the horizons of humanity into the cosmos in a manner reflective of shared aspirations.

As we anticipate future explorations that involve mining asteroids or establishing bases on other celestial bodies, the potential for leveraging in-situ resources becomes critical. Linux-powered systems will manage the intelligent extraction and utilization of these resources, ensuring that we can sustain long-duration missions and work toward the goals of off-world colonization. This commitment to resource efficiency aligns with the core values of sustainability, allowing humanity to maximize the use of available materials while safeguarding the integrity of extraterrestrial environments.

Security, as we move towards an era of increased interconnectedness between the systems on Mars, will be paramount. Linux's focus on robust cybersecurity measures represents a proactive approach to protecting mission-critical systems and the data they generate. The increasing reliance on data sharing and communication among interconnected robotic systems and habitats underscores the necessity for strong security protocols, ensuring that our explorations can continue uninhibited by threats from various realms.

Finally, the visionary future of Linux in space is characterized by humanity's growing understanding of our place in the cosmos and a commitment to exploring our universe responsibly. The next decades will see enhanced scientific pursuits as we utilize Linux as a powerful facilitator for uncovering the mysteries of life beyond Earth. The ongoing collaboration will drive our collective understanding of planetary systems, environmental dynamics, and potentially, the existence of life elsewhere.

In conclusion, the future of Linux in space holds immense promise, driven by its adaptability, community-driven development, and focus on collaboration. As we lay the groundwork for a new era of space exploration, we will leverage the strengths of Linux to create resilient, intelligent, and interconnected systems that empower humanity to reach new frontiers. The quest for knowledge beyond our planet is not merely a scientific endeavor; it is a testament to our ambitions, our ingenuity, and the unwavering spirit of exploration that defines humanity. As we venture into this extraordinary journey, Linux will undoubtedly be at the heart of our interconnected efforts in the vast expanse of the universe, guiding us toward a future of discovery and enlightenment.

www.ingramcontent.com/pod-product-compliance
Lightning Source LLC
LaVergne TN
LVHW051344050326
832903LV00031B/3742